WHAT'S COOKING
Thai

Christine France

THUNDER BAY
P·R·E·S·S

First published in the United States in 2000 by
Thunder Bay Press
An imprint of the Advantage Publishers Group
5880 Oberlin Drive, San Diego, CA 92121-4794
www.advantagebooksonline.com

A Parragon book, Parragon, Queen Street House, 4 Queen Street, Bath BA1 1HE, UK

Library of Congress Cataloging in Publication Data
France, Christine
    What's cooking : Thai / Christine France.
        p. cm.
    Includes index.
    ISBN 1-57145-256-7
        1. Cookery, Thai. 1.Title: Thai. 11. Title
    TX724.5.T5 F73 2000
    641.59593--dc21   00-023983
Printed in China
3 4 01 02 03
Produced by Haldane Mason, London

Acknowledgments
Editorial Consultant: Felicity Jackson
Photography: Colin Bowling, Paul Forrester, and Stephen Brayne
Home Economists and Stylist: David Morgan, Mandy Phipps, Gina Steer
All props supplied by Barbara Stewart at Surfaces.

NOTE

Unless otherwise stated, milk is assumed to be full fat,
eggs are medium, and pepper is freshly ground black pepper.

Recipes using uncooked eggs should be
avoided by infants, the elderly, pregnat women, and anyone
suffering from an illness

Contents

Introduction

Anyone who has a love of Thai food will appreciate that it is a unique cuisine, distinctly different from the countries which border it geographically, but with many clear foreign influences. Many of its characteristics are due to climate and culture, but a history of many centuries of invasions and emigration has played a large part in shaping Thai cuisine.

The roots of the Thai nation can be traced back to the first century, in the time of the Chinese Han Dynasty, when the T'ai tribes occupied parts of South China, along valuable trade routes between the East and West. Over the years, the T'ai had a close but often stormy relationship with the Chinese, and eventually began to emigrate South to the lands of what is now North Thailand, bordering Burma and Cambodia, then sparsely occupied by Buddhist and Hindu tribes.

Eventually, the T'ai established the independent Kingdom of Sukhothai (translated as 'dawn of happiness'), eventually known as Siam. The ports of Siam formed the entry to an important trade route, where ships from all over Europe and Japan docked in the coastal ports or sailed up the rivers bringing foreign foods, teas, and spices, silks, copper, and ceramics. It was the Portuguese who, in the sixteenth century, introduced the chili to this part of the world, where the plants thrived and continue to thrive. Trade with Arab and Indian merchants was important, too, and many muslims settled in Siam. The Kingdom of Siam survived until the twentieth century, when in 1939 it became the constitutional monarchy of Thailand.

Present-day Thailand still reflects much of these centuries of mixed cultures, and the Thai people are independent, proud, creative, and passionate. Their love of life is clear in the way they take pleasure in eating and entertaining. They love to eat, at any time of day, and the streets are lined with food vendors selling a huge variety of tasty snacks from their stalls, carts or bicycles all day long.

Thai people love parties and celebrations, and during their many festivals, the colorful, often elaborate and carefully prepared festive foods show a respect for custom and tradition. Visitors are entertained with endless trays of tasty snacks, platters of exotic fruits, and Thai beer or local whisky. When a meal is served, all the dishes are served up together, so the cook can enjoy the food along with the guests. Thais take pride in presenting food beautifully, often carving vegetables into elaborate shapes as garnish. Their intricate and skilled artistry is an important part of Thai culture, and shows a deep appreciaton of beautiful things.

Everyday life in Thailand is closely tied to the seasons, marked by the harvesting of crops and vagaries of the monsoon climate. The Thai people take their food seriously, taking great care in choosing the freshest ingredients and carefully balancing delicate flavors and textures. Throughout Thailand, rice is the most important, staple food, the center of every meal, and coconut in its various forms has an almost equal place. Cooks in every region are expert at making the very most of the food that's locally available, so the character of many classic Thai dishes will often vary depending on the region.

FUNDAMENTALS OF THAI CUISINE

Essential ingredients when you're starting out to cook your own Thai cuisine are coconut, lime, chili, rice, garlic, lemon grass, ginger, and cilantro, and with a basic supply of these you can create many typical Thai dishes. Although many recipes have long lists of ingredients, the methods are mostly simple enough for even an inexperienced cook to handle.

The main principle of Thai cooking is balance, the five extremes of flavor of bitter, sour, hot, salt, and sweet being carefully and skillfully balanced within a dish, or over several courses, each dish contributing part of the whole perfect balance of the entire meal.

4

TYPICAL THAI FLAVOURINGS:

BASIL

Three types of sweet basil are used in Thai cooking, but the sweet basil we can buy in the West also works well. Asian food stores often sell the seeds for Thai basil, so you can grow your own.

CHILIES

The many varieties of chili vary in heat, from very mild to fiery hot, so choose carefully. The small red or green "bird's eye" chilies often used in Thai dishes are very hot, so if you prefer a mild heat, remove the seeds. Red are generally slightly sweeter and milder than green. Larger chilies tend to be milder. Dried crushed chilies are used for seasoning.

COCONUT MILK

This is made from grated and pressed fresh coconut. Can be bought in cans, in powdered form or in blocks (creamed coconut). Coconut cream is skimmed from the top, and is slightly thicker and richer.

CILANTRO

This is a fresh herb with a pungent, citrus-like flavor, widely used in savory dishes. Try to buy it with a root attached.

GALANGAL

A relative of ginger with a milder, aromatic flavor. Available fresh or dried.

GARLIC

Used whole, crushed, sliced or chopped in savory dishes and curry pastes. Pickled garlic is another useful item and makes an attractive garnish.

GINGER

Fresh ginger is peeled and grated, chopped or sliced for a warm spicy flavor.

KAFFIR LIME LEAVES

The leaves have a distinctive lime scent, and can be bought fresh, dried or frozen.

LEMON GRASS

An aromatic tropical grass with a lemony scent similar to lemon balm. Strip off the fibrous outer leaves and slice or finely chop the rest, or bruise and use whole. Can also be bought in dried powdered form.

PALM SUGAR

This is a rich, brown unrefined sugar from the coconut palm, sold in solid blocks, and the best way to use it is to crush with a mallet or rolling pin. Dark brown sugar is an acceptable substitute.

RICE VINEGAR

Also called "mirin" this sweet rice vinegar is used as a savory flavoring. Sherry or white wine vinegar can be used as a substitute.

SOY SAUCE

Both dark and light soy sauces are used for seasoning, but light is saltier than dark. Light soy sauce is used mainly is stir-fries, or with light meats. Dark soy sauce adds a mature rich flavor and color to braised and red meat dishes.

TAMARIND PASTE

The pulp of the tamarind fruit, usually sold in blocks. This gives a sour/sweet flavor. Soak the pulp in hot water for 30 minutes, press out the juice and discard the pulp and seeds.

THAI FISH SAUCE

Called *nam pla,* this is used like salt for seasoning, and has a distinctive intense aroma. Made from salted, fermented fish.

Snacks, & Starters, Soups

The structure of a Thai meal is more flexible than in the West, with no starters and main courses as such; instead, soups, side dishes, noodles, rice, and main dishes appear simultaneously. Small snacks or appetizers may be served as afternoon snacks or offered to guests before they sit down for a meal.

Many of the recipes in this section are savory snacks that are eaten at all times of day and at parties and celebrations. The Thais eat when they are hungry, and street vendors cater for this need with a huge and tempting array of wares from their stalls and bicycles—each street vendor has his own speciality of fast food, from crab cakes to spare ribs, and steamed mussels to rice soup.

Soups are part of almost every Thai meal, including breakfast. Lunch is often a bowl of hearty soup, often thin stock-based broths, usually spiked with red or green chilies, and with the addition of fine noodles, rice, egg strips, or tiny fish balls, meat balls or cubes of tofu. In restaurants, soups are often served in a large "firepots" with a central funnel of burning coals to keep the contents hot.

Jumbo Shrimp Rolls with Sweet Soy Sauce

These crisp, golden-fried little mouthfuls are packed with flavor and served with a hot-and-sweet soy dip—perfect to stimulate appetites at the start of a meal, or as a tasty hot snack.

Serves 4

INGREDIENTS

DIP:
1 small red bird's eye chili, deseeded
1 tsp. honey
4 tbsp. soy sauce

ROLLS:
2 tbsp. chopped fresh cilantro
1 garlic clove
1½ tsp. red curry paste
16 wonton wrappers

1 egg white, lightly beaten
16 raw peeled jumbo shrimp with
 tails
sunflower oil for deep frying

1 To make the dip, finely chop the chili, then mix with the honey and soy and stir well; set aside.

2 To make the shrimp rolls, finely chop the cilantro and garlic and mix with the curry paste.

3 Brush each wonton wrapper with egg white and place a small dab of the cilantro mixture in the center. Place a shrimp on top and fold over, enclosing the shrimp and leaving the tail exposed. Repeat with the other shrimp.

4 Heat the oil to 350° F, or until a cube of bread turns golden brown in 30 seconds. Fry the shrimp in small batches for 1–2 minutes each until golden brown and crisp. Drain on paper towels and serve with the dip.

VARIATIONS

If you prefer, replace the wonton wrappers with phyllo pastry—use a long strip of phyllo pastry, place the paste and a shrimp on one end, then brush with egg white and wrap the pastry around the jumbo shrimp to enclose and fry.

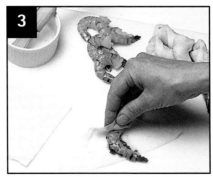

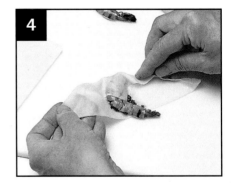

Shrimp & Chicken Sesame Toasts

*A popular delicacy found throughout many countries in the East, these crisp,
golden fried toasts are very simple to make and perfect to serve with drinks at parties.*

Makes 72 pieces

INGREDIENTS

4 boneless, skinless chicken thighs	1 tbsp. Thai fish sauce	shredded scallion curls, to garnish
3½ oz. cooked peeled shrimp	½ tsp. black pepper	
1 small egg, beaten	¼ tsp. salt	
3 scallions, finely chopped	12 slices white bread, crusts removed	
2 garlic cloves, crushed	8 tbsp. sesame seeds	
2 tbsp. chopped fresh cilantro	sunflower oil for pan-frying	

1 Place the chicken and shrimp in a food processor and process until very finely chopped. Add the egg, scallions, garlic, cilantro, fish sauce, pepper, and salt and pulse for a few seconds to mix well.

2 Spread the mixture evenly over the slices of bread, right to the edges. Scatter the sesame seeds over a plate and press the spread side of each slice of bread into them to coat evenly.

3 Using a sharp knife, cut the bread into small rectangles, making about 6 per slice.

4 Heat a ½ inch depth of oil in a wide frying pan until very hot. Quickly fry the bread triangles in batches for 2–3 minutes until golden brown, turning them over once.

5 Drain the toasts well on paper towels and serve hot, garnished with thinly shredded scallion curls.

COOK'S TIP

If you're catering for a party, it's a good idea to make the toasts in advance, then store them in the refrigerator or freezer. Cover and refrigerate for up to 3 days, or place in a sealed container or plastic bag and freeze for up to 1 month. Thaw overnight in the refrigerator, then pop into a hot oven for about 5 minutes to reheat thoroughly.

Thai Fish Cakes with Hot Peanut Dip

These little fish cakes are very popular in Thailand as street food, and make a perfect snack. Or, serve them as an appetizer, complete with the spicy peanut dip.

Serves 4–5

INGREDIENTS

12 oz. white fish fillet without skin, such as cod or haddock
1 tbsp. Thai fish sauce
2 tsp. red curry paste
1 tbsp. lime juice
1 garlic clove, crushed
4 dried kaffir lime leaves, crumbled

1 egg white
3 tbsp. chopped fresh cilantro
salt and pepper
vegetable oil for pan-frying
green salad leaves, to serve

PEANUT DIP:
1 small red chili
1 tbsp. light soy sauce
1 tbsp. lime juice
1 tbsp. soft light brown sugar
3 tbsp. chunky peanut butter
4 tbsp. coconut milk

1 Put the fish fillet in a food processor with the fish sauce, curry paste, lime juice, garlic, lime leaves, and egg white and process until a smooth paste forms.

2 Stir in the cilantro and quickly process again until mixed. Divide the mixture in to 8–10 pieces and roll into balls, then

flatten to make round patties and set aside.

3 For the dip, halve and deseed the chili, then chop finely. Place in a small pan with the remaining dip ingredients and heat gently, stirring constantly, until well blended. Adjust the seasoning to taste.

4 Pan-fry the fish cakes in batches for 3–4 minutes on each side until golden brown. Drain on paper towels and serve hot on a bed of green salad leaves with the chili-flavored peanut dip.

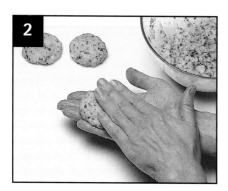

Steamed Crab Cakes

These pretty little steamed and fried crab cakes are usually served as a snack, but you can serve them as an appetizer instead. In Thailand the banana leaves are skillfully shaped to make a container, but for ease of use we've used ramekins.

Serves 4

INGREDIENTS

1–2 banana leaves*
2 garlic cloves, crushed
1 tsp. finely chopped lemon grass
½ tsp. ground black pepper
2 tbsp. fresh chopped fresh cilantro
3 tbsp. creamed coconut

1 tbsp. lime juice
1 cup cooked crab meat, flaked
1 tbsp. Thai fish sauce
2 egg whites
1 egg yolk
8 fresh cilantro leaves

sunflower oil for deep frying
chili sauce dip, to serve

Most Asian stores sell banana leaves, but waxed paper can be substituted.

1 Use the banana leaves to line eight 100 ml (scant ½ cup) ramekins or foil containers.

2 Mix together the garlic, lemon grass, black pepper and cilantro. Mash with the creamed coconut with the lime juice until smooth. Stir it into the other ingredients with the crab meat and fish sauce.

3 In a clean, dry bowl, whisk the egg whites until stiff, then lightly and evenly fold them into the crab mixture.

4 Spoon the mixture into the lined containers and press down lightly. Brush the tops with egg yolk and top each with a cilantro leaf.

5 Place in a steamer half-filled with boiling water, then cover with a lid and steam for 15 minutes, or until firm to the touch. Pour off the excess liquid and remove from the ramekins or foil containers.

6 Heat the oil to 350° F, or until a cube of bread browns in 30 seconds. Add the crab cakes and deep fry for about 1 minute, turning them over once, until golden brown. Serve hot with a chili sauce dip.

Thai-style
Open Crab Meat Sandwich

A hearty, open sandwich, topped with a classic flavor combination—
crab with avocado and ginger. Perfect for a light summer lunch—or anytime!

Serves 2

INGREDIENTS

2 tbsp. lime juice

3/4 in. piece fresh ginger, grated

3/4 in. piece lemon grass, finely
chopped

5 tbsp. mayonnaise

2 large slices crusty bread

1 ripe avocado

1 cup cooked crab meat

sprigs fresh cilantro, to garnish

1 Mix half the lime juice with the ginger and lemon grass. Add the mayonnaise and mix well.

2 Spread 1 tablespoon mayonnaise over each slice of bread.

3 Halve the avocado and remove the pit. Peel and slice the flesh thinly, then arrange the slices on the bread. Sprinkle with lime juice.

4 Spoon the crab meat over the avocado, then add any remaining lime juice. Spoon over the remaining mayonnaise, top with a cilantro sprig and serve immediately

COOK'S TIP
To make lime- and ginger-flavored mayonnaise, place 2 egg yolks, 1 tablespoon lime juice, and ½ teaspoon grated ginger in a blender. With the motor running, gradually add 1¼ cups olive oil, drop by drop, until the mixture is thick and smooth. Season with salt and pepper.

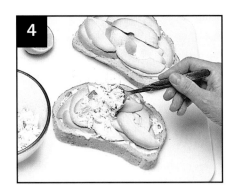

Mussels in Spiced Batter

Little taste explosions—these make excellent nibbles to have with drinks before a meal, as they really pep up appetites, and leave everyone wanting more.

Serves 4

INGREDIENTS

40 large fresh mussels in shell
2 tbsp. all-purpose flour
2 tbsp. rice flour
½ tsp. salt
1 tbsp. dried coconut flakes

1 egg white
1 tbsp. rice wine
2 tbsp. water
1 small red bird's eye chili, deseeded
   and chopped

1 tbsp. chopped fresh cilantro
sunflower oil for deep frying
lime wedges, to serve

1   Clean the mussels thoroughly and discard any that are damaged or do not close when tapped. Rinse in cold water and place in a pan with just the water clinging to them, cover and steam over a high heat for 2–3 minutes, shaking the pan occasionally, until the mussels open. Drain, then remove from the shells. Discard any that are not open.

2   For the batter, sift the all-purpose flour, rice flour, and salt into a bowl. Add the coconut, egg white, rice wine and water and beat until well mixed and a batter forms. Stir the chili and cilantro into the batter.

3   Heat a 2 in. depth of oil in a large pan to 350° F, or until a cube of bread browns in 30 seconds. Holding the mussels with a fork, dip them quickly into the batter, then drop into the hot oil and fry for 1–2 minutes until crisp and golden brown.

4   Drain the mussels on paper towels and serve hot with lime wedges to squeeze over.

COOK'S TIP

If you reserve the mussel shells, the cooked mussels can be replaced in them to serve.

Steamed Mussels with Lemon Grass & Basil

Thai cooks are fond of basil, and frequently sprinkle it over salads and soups. The familiar sweet basil available in Europe and America is ideal for use in most Thai recipes, including this one.

Serves 4

INGREDIENTS

2 lb. 4 oz. fresh mussels in shell	2 tbsp. lime juice	crusty bread, to serve
2 shallots, finely chopped	1 tbsp. Thai fish sauce	
1 lemon grass stalk, finely sliced	2 tbsp. butter	
1 garlic clove, finely chopped	4 tbsp. chopped fresh basil	
3 tbsp. rice wine or sherry	salt and pepper	

1 Clean the mussels, removing any beards and dirt. Rinse in clear water and drain. Discard any which will not close when tapped, or have damaged shells.

2 Place the shallots, lemon grass, garlic, rice wine, lime juice, and fish sauce in a large pan and place over a high heat.

3 Add the mussels, cover with a lid and steam the mussels for 2–3 minutes, shaking the pan occasionally until the mussels open.

4 Discard any mussels which have not opened, then stir in the chopped basil and season with salt and pepper.

5 Scoop out the mussels with a perforated spoon and divide between 4 deep bowls. Quickly whisk the butter into the pan juices, then pour the juices over the mussels.

6 Serve with plenty of crusty bread to mop up the juices.

COOK'S TIP
If you prefer to serve this dish as a main course, this amount will be enough to serve two portions. Fresh clams in shell are also very good cooked by this method.

Roasted Spare Ribs with Honey & Soy

Ideally, ask your butcher to chop the spare ribs into short lengths, about 2½ inches long, so they're easy to eat with your fingers.

Serves 4

INGREDIENTS

2 lb. 4 oz. Chinese-style spare ribs	1 small onion, chopped	2 tbsp. honey
½ lemon	2 tbsp. soy sauce	1 tbsp. sesame oil
½ small orange	2 tbsp. rice wine	
1 in. piece fresh ginger, peeled	½ tsp. Thai seven-spice powder	
2 garlic cloves, peeled		

1 Place the ribs in a wide roasting pan, cover loosely with foil and cook in an oven preheated to 350° F for 30 minutes.

2 Meanwhile, remove any seeds from the lemon and orange and place in a food processor with the ginger, garlic, onion, soy sauce, rice wine, seven-spice powder, honey, and sesame oil. Process until smooth.

3 Pour off any fat from the spare ribs, then spoon the puréed mixture over the spare ribs. Toss the ribs to coat evenly.

4 Return the ribs to the oven at 400° F and roast for about 40 minutes, turning and basting them occasionally, or until golden brown. Serve hot.

COOK'S TIP

If you don't have a food processor, grate the rind and squeeze the juice from the citrus fruits, grate the ginger, crush the garlic, and finely chop the onion. Mix these ingredients together with the remaining ingredients.

Steamed Wonton Bundles

These little steamed dumplings are served as a first course with a spicy dip. It's worth making a large batch and keeping a few in the freezer to thaw and cook as you need them.

Serves 4

INGREDIENTS

4½ oz. ground pork
1 tbsp. dried shrimp, finely chopped
1 green chili, finely chopped
2 shallots, finely chopped

1 tsp. cornstarch
1 small egg, beaten
2 tsp. dark soy sauce
2 tsp. rice wine

12 wonton wrappers
1 tsp. sesame oil
salt and pepper

1 Mix together the pork, shrimp, chili, and shallots. Blend the cornstarch with half the egg and stir into the pork mixture with the soy sauce and rice wine. Season to taste with salt and pepper.

2 Arrange the wonton wrappers flat on a work surface and place about 1 tablespoon of the pork mixture on to the center of each.

3 Brush the wrappers with the remaining egg and pull up the edges, pinching together lightly at the top, leaving a small gap so the filling can just be seen.

4 Bring water in the bottom of a steamer to a boil and brush the inside of the top part with sesame oil. Arrange the wontons in the top, over and steam for 15–20 minutes. Serve hot.

COOK'S TIP

Make sure that the water in the base of the steamer is not allowed to stop boiling, or the dumplings will be undercooked and soggy. Also keep an eye on it so it doesn't boil dry—refill with extra boiling water if necessary.

Crispy Pork and Peanut Baskets

These tasty little appetite-teasers are an adaptation of a traditional recipe in which Thai cooks make with a light batter, but phyllo pastry is a good substitute that is much easier to handle.

Serves 4

INGREDIENTS

2 sheets phyllo pastry, each about
   16½ x 11 inches
2 tbsp. vegetable oil
1 garlic clove, crushed

4½ oz. ground pork
1 tsp. red Thai curry paste
2 scallions, finely chopped
3 tbsp. crunchy peanut butter

1 tbsp. light soy sauce
1 tbsp. chopped fresh cilantro
salt and pepper

1 Cut each sheet of phyllo pastry into twenty-four 4 inch squares, to make a total of 48 squares. Brushing each square lightly with oil, arrange the squares in stacks of 4 in 12 small muffin pans, points outward. Press the pastry down into the pans.

2 Bake the pastry cases in the oven preheated to 400° F for 6–8 minutes until golden brown.

3 Meanwhile, heat 1 tablespoon oil in a wok. Add the garlic and fry for 30 seconds, then stir in the pork and stir-fry over a high heat for 4-5 minutes until golden brown.

4 Add the curry paste and scallions and stir-fry for 1 further minute, then stir in the peanut butter, soy sauce and cilantro. Season to taste with salt and pepper.

5 Spoon the pork mixture into the phyllo baskets and serve hot, as a first course.

COOK'S TIP
When using phyllo pastry, remember that it dries out very quickly and becomes brittle and difficult to handle, so work quickly and keep any sheets of pastry you're not using covered with plastic wrap and a dampened cloth.

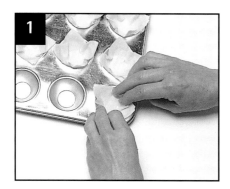

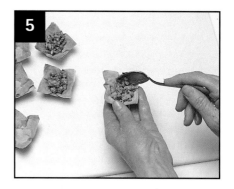

Sticky Ginger Chicken Wings

A finger-licking appetizer that's ideal for parties—but have ready some finger bowls.
If you can't get chicken wings for this recipe, use drumsticks instead.

Serves 4

INGREDIENTS

2 garlic cloves, peeled	2 tbsp. candied ginger syrup	1 tsp. sesame oil
1 piece candied ginger in syrup	2 tbsp. dark soy sauce	12 chicken wings
1 tsp. coriander seeds	1 tbsp. lime juice	

1 Roughly chop the garlic and ginger. In a mortar and pestle, crush the garlic, candied ginger, and coriander seeds to a paste, gradually working in the ginger syrup, soy sauce, lime juice, and sesame oil.

2 Tuck the pointed tip of each chicken wing underneath the thicker end to make a neat triangular shape. Place in a large bowl.

3 Add the garlic and ginger paste to the bowl and toss the chicken wings in the mixture to coat evenly. Cover and leave in the refrigerator to marinate for several hours or overnight.

4 Arrange the chicken wings in one layer on a foil-lined broiler pan and broil under a medium-hot broiler for 12–15 minutes, turning them occasionally, until golden brown and thoroughly cooked. Alternatively, cook on a lightly oiled barbecue grid over medium-hot coals for 12–15 minutes.

COOK'S TIP

To test if the chicken is cooked, pierce it deeply through the thickest part of the flesh. When fully cooked, the chicken juices are clear, with no trace of pink. If there is any trace of pink, cook for a few more minutes.

Stuffed Chicken Wings

The preparation of this dish is time-consuming, but is worth the effort. With their unusual, typically Thai savory stuffing, these can be served hot or cold, and make a delicious picnic dish.

Serves 4

INGREDIENTS

8 chicken wings
3 tbsp. dried shrimp
3 tbsp. hot water
7 oz. ground pork
1 garlic clove, peeled and crushed

1 tbsp. Thai fish sauce
½ tsp. salt
½ tsp. ground black pepper
2 scallions, finely chopped
¼ tsp. turmeric

1 small egg, beaten
2 tbsp. rice flour
sunflower oil for deep frying
sweet chili dipping sauce, to serve

1 Using a small sharp knife, cut around the end of the bone at the cut end of each wing, then loosen the flesh away from around the bone, scraping it downward with the knife and pulling back the skin as you go. When you reach the next joint, grasp the end of the bone and twist sharply to break it at the joint. Remove the bone and turn back the flesh.

2 Continue to scrape the meat away down the length of the next long bone, exposing the joint. Twist to break the bone at the joint and remove, leaving just the wing tip in place.

3 Meanwhile, soak the dried shrimp in the hot water for 10–15 minutes. Drain well, then chop finely. Place the pork, shrimp, garlic, fish sauce, salt, and pepper into a food processor and process until a fairly smooth paste forms. Add the scallions and stir well to mix.

4 Use the mixture to stuff the chicken wings, pressing it down inside with your finger.

5 Beat the turmeric into the egg. Dip each chicken wing into the rice flour, shaking off the excess.

6 Heat a 2 inch depth of oil in a large pan to 375° F, or until a cube of bread browns in 40 seconds. Dip the floured chicken wings quickly into the turmeric-flavored egg, then drop carefully into the hot oil and fry in small batches for about 8–10 minutes, turning them over once.

7 Drain on paper towels and serve hot or cold with a sweet chili dipping sauce.

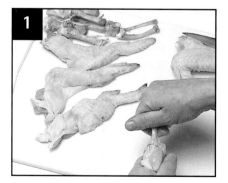

Lemon Grass Chicken Skewers

An unusual way to use fresh lemon grass stalks as skewers, which impart their delicate lemony flavor to the chicken mixture.

Serves 4

INGREDIENTS

2 long or 4 short lemon grass stalks
2 large boneless, skinless chicken
   breasts, about 14 oz. in total
1 small egg white
1 carrot, finely grated

1 small red chili, deseeded and
   chopped
2 tbsp. chopped fresh garlic chives
2 tbsp. chopped fresh cilantro
1 tbsp. sunflower oil

salt and pepper
cilantro and lime slices, to garnish

1 If the lemon grass stalks are long, cut them in half across the middle to make 4 short lengths. Cut each stalk in half lengthways, so you have 8 sticks.

2 Roughly chop the chicken pieces and place them in a food processor with the egg white. Process to a smooth paste, then add the carrot, chili, chives, cilantro, and salt and pepper. Process for a few seconds to mix well.

3 Chill the mixture in the refrigerator for about 15 minutes. Divide the mixture into 8 equal portions, and use your hands to shape the mixture around the lemon grass "skewers."

4 Brush the skewers and broil under a preheated medium-hot broiler for 4–6 minutes, turning them occasionally, until golden brown and thoroughly cooked. Alternatively, grill over medium-hot coals.

5 Serve hot, with cilantro and lime slices to garnish.

COOK'S TIP

If you can't find whole lemon grass stalks, use wooden or bamboo skewers instead, and add ½ teaspoon ground lemon grass to the mixture with the other flavorings.

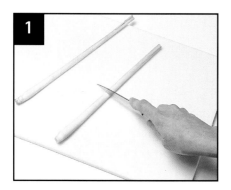

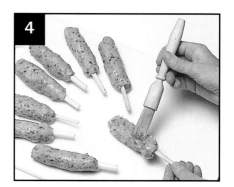

Chicken Roasted in Banana Leaves

Leaves such as banana are often used in Thai cooking as a natural wrapping for all kinds of ingredients. These tasty little appetizers will set everyone's taste buds jumping.

Serves 4–6

INGREDIENTS

1 garlic clove, chopped
1 tsp. finely chopped fresh ginger
$1/4$ tsp. ground black pepper
2 sprigs fresh cilantro

1 tbsp. Thai fish sauce
1 tbsp. whisky
3 boneless, skinless chicken breasts
2–3 banana leaves, cut into $1^1/4$ inch

wide strips
sunflower oil for pan-frying

1 Place the garlic, ginger, pepper, cilantro, fish sauce, and whisky in a mortar and pestle and grind to a smooth paste.

2 Cut the chicken into 1 inch chunks and toss with the paste to coat evenly. Cover and chill in the refrigerator to marinate for about 1 hour.

3 Place a piece of chicken on a square of banana leaf and wrap it up like a package to enclose the chicken completely. Secure with

wooden toothpicks or tie with bamboo string.

4 Heat a ⅛ inch depth of oil in a heavy-based frying pan until hot.

5 Fry the packets for 8–10 minutes, turning them over occasionally until golden brown and the chicken is thoroughly cooked. Serve with a sweet chili dipping sauce.

COOK'S TIP
To make a sweet chili dip to serve with the chicken pieces, mix together equal amounts of chili sauce and tomato ketchup, then stir in a dash of rice wine to taste.

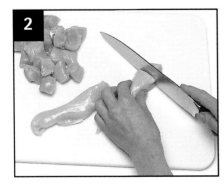

Chicken Balls with Dipping Sauce

Serve these bite-sized chicken appetizers warm as a snack or with drinks,
or packed cold for a picnic or lunchbox treat.

Serves 4

INGREDIENTS

2 large boneless, skinless chicken
  breasts
3 tbsp. vegetable oil
2 shallots, finely chopped
½ celery stick, finely chopped
1 garlic clove, crushed

2 tbsp. light soy sauce
1 small egg
1 bunch scallions
salt and pepper
scallion tassels, to garnish

DIPPING SAUCE:
3 tbsp. dark soy sauce
1 tbsp. rice wine
1 tsp. sesame seeds

1 Cut the chicken into ¾ inch pieces. Heat half of the oil in a wok and stir-fry the chicken quickly over a high heat for 2–3 minutes until golden. Remove the chicken from the wok with a perforated spoon and set aside.

2 Add the shallots, celery and garlic to the pan and stir-fry for 1–2 minutes until softened but not browned.

3 Place the chicken, shallots, celery, and garlic in a food processor and process until finely ground. Add 1 tablespoon of the light soy sauce and salt and pepper and just enough egg to make a fairly firm mixture.

4 Trim the scallions and cut into 2 inch lengths. Make the dipping sauce by mixing together the dark soy sauce, rice wine and sesame seeds; set aside.

5 Shape the chicken mixture into 16–18 walnut-sized balls. Heat the remaining oil in a wok and stir-fry the chicken balls in small batches for 4–5 minutes until golden brown. Drain on paper towels and keep hot.

6 Stir-fry the scallions for 1–2 minutes to soften, then stir in the remaining light soy sauce. Serve with the chicken balls and dipping sauce. Serve on a platter, garnished with scallion tassels.

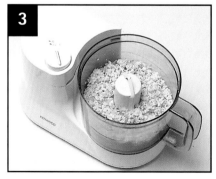

Stuffed Eggs
with Pork & Crab Meat

These savory stuffed eggs make a good picnic dish, or they can be popped into a lunchbox for an unusual treat. Cool the eggs completely before packing.

Serves 4

INGREDIENTS

4 large eggs
3½ oz. ground pork
6 oz. can white crab meat, drained
1 garlic clove, crushed
1 tsp. Thai fish sauce

½ tsp. ground lemon grass
1 tbsp. chopped fresh cilantro
1 tbsp. dried coconut flakes
⅔ cup all-purpose flour
about ⅔ cup coconut milk

salt and pepper
sunflower oil for deep frying
green salad, to serve

1 Place the eggs in a pan of simmering water and bring to a boil, then simmer for 10 minutes. Drain the eggs, crack the shells and cool under cold running water. Peel off the shells.

2 Cut the eggs in half lengthways and scoop out the yolks. Place the yolks in a bowl with the pork, crab meat, garlic, fish sauce, lemon grass, cilantro, and coconut. Season well with salt and pepper and mix the ingredients together thoroughly.

3 Divide the mixture into 8 equal portions, then fill each of the egg whites with the mixture, pressing together with your hands to form the shape of a whole egg.

4 Whisk together the flour and enough coconut milk to make a thick coating batter, seasoning with salt and pepper. Heat a 2 inch depth of oil in a large pan to 375° F, or until a cube of bread browns in 40 seconds. Dip each egg into the coconut batter, then shake off the excess and place it into the hot oil.

5 Fry the eggs in 2 batches for about 5 minutes, turning occasionally, until golden brown. Remove with a perforated spoon and drain on paper towels. Serve warm or cold with a green salad.

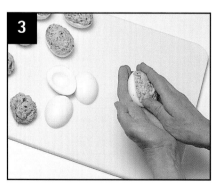

Thai-stuffed Omelette

*This makes a substantial appetizer, or a light lunch or supper dish.
Serve with a colorful, crisp salad to accompany the dish.*

Serves 4

INGREDIENTS

2 garlic cloves, chopped
4 black peppercorns
4 sprigs fresh cilantro
2 tbsp. vegetable oil

7 oz. ground pork
2 scallions, chopped
1 large, firm tomato, chopped
6 large eggs

1 tbsp. Thai fish sauce
$1/4$ tsp. turmeric
chopped fresh cilantro, to garnish

1 Place the garlic, peppercorns, and cilantro in a mortar and pestle and crush until a smooth paste forms.

2 Heat 1 tablespoon of the oil in a wok over a medium heat. Add the paste and and fry for 1–2 minutes until it just changes color.

3 Stir in the pork and stir-fry until it is lightly browned. Add the scallion and tomato and stir-fry for a further minute, then remove from the heat.

4 Heat the remaining oil in a small, heavy-based frying pan. Beat the eggs with the fish sauce and turmeric, then pour a quarter of the egg mixture into the pan. As the mixture begins to set, stir lightly to ensure all the liquid egg is set.

5 Spoon a quarter of the pork mixture down the center of the omelette, then fold the sides inward toward the center, enclosing the filling. Make 3 more omelettes with the remaining egg and fill with the remaining pork mixture.

6 Slide the omelettes on to a serving plate and sprinkle with chopped fresh cilantro to serve.

COOK'S TIP

If you prefer, spread half the pork mixture evenly over one omelette, then place a second omelette on top, without folding. Cut into slim wedges to serve.

Vegetarian Spring Rolls

These bite-sized vegetarian noodle-filled rolls are a tasty appetizer
to serve at the start of any meal, with a sweet chili dip.

Serves 4

INGREDIENTS

1 oz. fine cellophane noodles

2 tbsp. peanut oil

2 garlic cloves, crushed

½ tsp. grated fresh ginger

⅔ cup oyster mushrooms, thinly
    sliced

2 scallions, finely chopped

½ cup bean sprouts

1 small carrot, finely shredded

½ tsp. sesame oil

1 tbsp. light soy sauce

1 tbsp. rice wine or dry sherry

¼ tsp. ground black pepper

1 tbsp. chopped fresh cilantro

1 tbsp. chopped fresh mint

24 spring- (egg-) roll wrappers

½ tsp. cornstarch

peanut oil for deep frying

1 Place the noodles in a heatproof bowl, pour over enough boiling water to cover and leave to stand for 4 minutes. Drain, rinse in cold water, then drain again. Cut into 2 inch lengths.

2 Heat the peanut oil in a wok or wide pan over a high heat. Add the garlic, ginger, oyster mushrooms, bean sprouts, and carrot and stir-fry for about 1 minute until just softened.

3 Stir in the sesame oil, soy sauce, rice wine, pepper, cilantro, and mint, then remove from the heat. Stir in the rice noodles.

4 Arrange the spring- (egg-) roll wrappers on a work surface, pointing diagonally. Mix the cornstarch with 1 tablespoon water and brush the edges of 1 wrapper with this. Spoon a little filling on to one pointed side of a wrapper.

5 Roll the point of the wrapper over the filling, then fold the side points inward over the filling. Continue to roll up the wrapper away from you, moistening the tip with more cornstarch mixture to secure to the roll.

6 Heat the oil in a wok or deep frying pan to 350° F, or until a cube of bread browns in 30 seconds. Add rolls in batches and deep fry for 2–3 minutes each until golden brown and crisp. Serve hot.

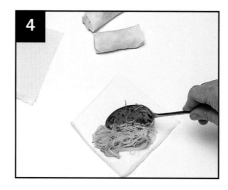

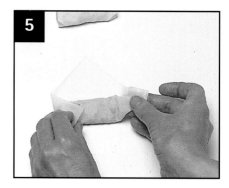

Sweet-Sour Seafood Salad

This unusual seafood dish with a sweet lime dressing can be either a starter or doubled up for a buffet-style main dish, and is a good dish to prepare for a crowd if you're entertaining.

Serves 6 as an appetizer

INGREDIENTS

18 fresh mussels in shell
6 large scallops
7 oz. baby squid, cleaned
2 shallots, finely chopped
6 raw jumbo shrimp, peeled and
  deveined

$1/4$ cucumber
1 carrot, peeled
$1/4$ head Chinese cabbage, shredded

DRESSING:
4 tbsp. lime juice

2 garlic cloves, finely chopped
2 tbsp. Thai fish sauce
1 tsp. sesame oil
1 tbsp. soft light brown sugar
2 tbsp. chopped fresh mint
$1/4$ tsp. ground black pepper
salt

1 Clean the mussels, discarding any damaged or open ones that do not close when firmly tapped. Steam them in just the water which clings to them for 1–2 minutes until opened. Lift out with a perforated spoon, reserving the liquid in the pan. Discard any mussels that have not opened.

2 Separate the corals from the scallops and cut the whites in half horziontally. Cut the tentacles from the squid and slice the body cavities into rings.

3 Add the shallots to the liquid in the pan and simmer over a high heat until the liquid is reduced to about 3 tablespoons. Add the scallops, squid, and jumbo shrimp and stir for 2–3 minutes until cooked. Remove and spoon into a wide bowl.

4 Cut the cucumber and carrot in half lengthways, then slice thinly on a diagonal angle to make long, pointed slices. Toss with the Chinese cabbage.

5 To make the dressing, place all the ingredients in a screw-top jar and shake well until evenly combined. Season to taste with salt and pepper.

6 Toss the vegetables and seafood together and spoon over the dressing. Serve immediately.

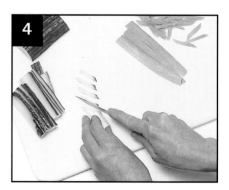

Warm Salad of Tuna & Tomatoes with Ginger Dressing

A colorful, refreshing first course that is perfect to make for a special summer lunch or dinner. The dressing can be made in advance and spooned over just before serving.

Serves 4

INGREDIENTS

½ cup Chinese cabbage, shredded
3 tbsp. rice wine
2 tbsp. Thai fish sauce
1 tbsp. finely shredded fresh ginger
1 garlic clove, finely chopped
½ small bird's eye red chili, finely

chopped
2 tsp. soft light brown sugar
2 tbsp. lime juice
400 g/14 oz. fresh tuna steak
sunflower oil for brushing
125 g/4½ oz/1 cup cherry tomatoes

roughly chopped fresh mint leaves, to garnish

1 Place a small pile of shredded Chinese cabbage on serving plates. Place the rice wine, fish sauce, ginger, garlic, chili, brown sugar and 1 tablespoon lime juice in a jar and shake well to combine evenly.

2 Cut the tuna into strips of an even thickness. Sprinkle with the remaining lime juice.

3 Brush a griddle or wide frying pan with the oil and heat until very hot. Arrange the tuna strips on the pan and cook until just firm and light golden, turning them over once. Remove and set aside.

4 Add the tomatoes to the pan and cook over a high heat until lightly browned. Spoon the tuna and tomatoes over the Chinese cabbage and spoon over the dressing. Scatter with chopped fresh mint and serve warm.

COOK'S TIP
You can make a quick version of this dish using canned tuna. There's no need to cook, instead just drain and flake the tuna, omit steps 2 and 3, and continue as in the recipe.

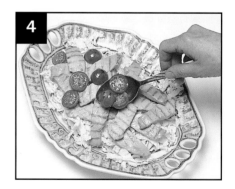

Chili-spiced Shrimp Wonton Soup

This delicious soup has a real kick of red-hot chilies, perfect to warm up a winter's day.
If you prefer a milder flavor, remove the seeds from the chilies before using them.

Serves 4

INGREDIENTS

WONTONS:
6 oz. cooked peeled shrimp
1 garlic clove, crushed
1 scallion, finely chopped
1 tbsp. dark soy sauce
1 tbsp. Thai fish sauce
1 tbsp. chopped fresh cilantro

1 small egg, separated
12 wonton wrappers

SOUP:
2 small red bird's eye chilies
2 scallions
4 cups clear beef stock

1 tbsp. Thai fish sauce
1 tbsp. dark soy sauce
1 tbsp. rice wine
handful of cilantro leaves, to garnish

1 Finely chop the shrimp. Put them in a bowl and stir in the garlic, scallion, soy sauce, fish sauce, cilantro, and egg yolk.

2 Lay the wonton wrappers on a work surface in a single layer and place about 1 tablespoon of the filling mixture into the middle of each. Brush the edges with egg white and fold each one into a triangle, pressing lightly to seal.

Bring the 2 bottom corners of the triangle around to meet in the middle, securing with a little egg white to hold in place.

3 For the soup, slice the chilies on a steep diagonal angle to make long slices, removing the seeds if you prefer. Slice the scallions on the same angle.

4 Place the stock, fish sauce, soy sauce and rice wine in a large pan and bring to a boil. Add the chilies and scallions. Drop the wontons into the pan and simmer for 4–5 minutes until thoroughly heated.

5 Serve the soup and wontons in small bowls, garnish with fresh cilantro leaves scattered over at the last moment.

Hot & Sour Soup

Hot-and-sour mixtures are popular throughout the East, especially in Thailand. This soup typically has either shrimp or chicken added, but tofu could be used instead if you prefer a meatless version.

Serves 4

INGREDIENTS

12 oz. whole raw or cooked shrimp in shell
1 tbsp. vegetable oil
1 lemon grass stalk, roughly chopped
2 kaffir lime leaves, shredded
1 green chili, deseeded and chopped

5 cups chicken or fish stock
1 lime
1 tbsp. Thai fish sauce
salt and pepper
1 red bird's eye chili, deseeded and sliced

1 scallion, thinly sliced
1 tbsp. chopped cilantro, to garnish

1 Peel the shrimp and reserve the shells. Devein the shrimp, cover and chill until needed.

2 Heat the oil in a large pan and stir-fry the shrimp shells for 3–4 minutes until they turn pink. Add the lemon grass, lime leaves, chili and stock. Pare a strip of zest from the lime and add to the pan.

3 Bring to a boil, then lower the heat, cover and simmer for about 20 minutes.

4 Strain the liquid and pour it back into the pan. Squeeze the juice from the lime and add to the pan with the fish sauce and salt and pepper to taste.

5 Return to a boil, the lower the heat, add the shrimp and simmer for 2-3 minutes.

6 Add the thinly sliced chili and scallion. Sprinkle with cilantro and serve.

COOK'S TIP

To devein the shrimp, remove the shells. Cut a slit along the back of each shrimp and remove the fine black vein that runs along the length of the back. Wipe with paper towels.

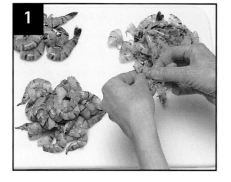

Creamy Corn Soup with Egg

This speedy soup is a good pantry standby, made in a matter of minutes.
If you prefer, you can use frozen crab sticks, thawed and chopped,
or cooked shrimp instead of canned crab meat.

Serves 4

INGREDIENTS

1 tbsp. vegetable oil
3 garlic cloves, crushed
1 tsp. grated fresh ginger
3 cups chicken stock

13 oz. can creamed corn
1 tbsp. Thai fish sauce
6 oz. can white crab meat, drained
1 egg

salt and pepper
chopped fresh cilantro and paprika, to
    garnish

1 Heat the oil in large saucepan and fry the crushed garlic for 1 minute, stirring constantly.

2 Add the ginger to the pan, then stir in the stock and creamed corn. Bring to a boil.

3 Stir in the fish sauce, crab meat, and salt and pepper, then return the soup to a boil.

4 Beat the egg, then stir lightly into the soup so it sets into long strands. Simmer gently for about 30 seconds until just set.

5 Ladle the soup into bowls and serve hot, garnished with chopped cilantro and paprika pepper sprinkled over.

COOK'S TIP
To give the soup an extra rich flavor kick for a special occasion, stir in 1 tablespoon of dry sherry or rice wine just before you ladle it into bowls.

Pumpkin & Coconut Soup

This substantial soup is filling, and if served with crusty bread is all you need for a satisfying lunch.
For a first course, serve in small bowls with a spoonful of spicy relish stirred into each portion.

Serves 6

INGREDIENTS

2 lb. 4 oz. pumpkin

1 tbsp. peanut oil

1 tsp. yellow mustard seeds

1 garlic clove, crushed

1 large onion, chopped

1 celery stick, chopped

1 small red chili, chopped

3³/₄ cups chicken stock

1 tbsp. dried shrimp

5 tbsp. coconut cream

salt and pepper

chopped fresh cilantro, to garnish

1 Halve the pumpkin and remove the seeds. Cut away the skin and dice the flesh.

2 Heat the oil in a large pan and fry the mustard seeds until they begin to pop. Stir in the garlic, onion, celery, and chili and stir-fry for 1–2 minutes.

3 Add the pumpkin with the stock and dried shrimp and bring to a boil. Lower the heat, cover and simmer gently for about 30 minutes until the ingredients are very tender.

4 Transfer the mixture to a food processor or blender and process until smooth. Return to the pan and stir in the coconut cream. Adjust the seasoning to taste with salt and pepper and serve hot, sprinkled with chopped cilantro.

COOK'S TIP

For an extra touch of garnish, swirl a spoonful of thick coconut milk into each bowl of soup as you serve it.

Mushroom & Tofu Broth

Dried black mushrooms are sold in Asian stores, and although they can be expensive they are worth searching out as they have a very specific aroma and flavor.

Serves 4

INGREDIENTS

4 cups rich brown stock
4 dried black mushrooms
1½ cups fresh oyster mushrooms, sliced
1 tbsp. sunflower oil
1 tsp. sesame oil

1 garlic clove, crushed
1 green chili, deseeded and finely chopped
6 scallions
2 kaffir lime leaves, finely shredded
2 tbsp. lime juice

1 tbsp. rice vinegar
1 tbsp. Thai fish sauce
½ cup firm tofu, diced
salt and pepper

1 Pour ⅔ cup boiling water over the mushrooms in a heatproof bowl and leave to soak for about 30 minutes. Drain, reserving the liquid, then chop the mushrooms roughly.

2 Heat the sunflower and sesame oils in a work over a high heat. Add the garlic, chili and scallions and stir-fry for 1 minute until softened but not browned.

3 Add the drained black and oyster mushrooms, kaffir lime leaves, stock and reserved mushroom liquid. Bring to a boil.

4 Stir in the lime juice, rice vinegar and fish sauce, lower the heat and simmer gently for 3–4 minutes.

5 Add the diced tofu and adjust the seasoning to taste with salt and pepper. Heat gently until boiling, then serve immediately.

COOK'S TIP

Use a clear, richly colored homemade beef stock, or alternatively a Japanese dashi, to make an attractive clear broth. Bouillon cubes generally make a cloudy stock. To make a vegetarian version of the broth, use a well-flavored vegetable stock and replace the fish sauce with light soy sauce.

Rice Soup with Eggs

This version of a classic Thai soup, sometimes eaten for breakfast, is a good way of using up any leftover cooked rice, especially when you've cooked too much.

Serves 4

INGREDIENTS

1 tsp. sunflower oil
1 garlic clove, crushed
1³/₄ oz. ground pork
3 scallions, sliced
1 tbsp. grated fresh ginger

1 red bird's eye chili, deseeded and
    chopped
4 cups chicken stock
1¹/₄ cups cooked long-grain rice
1 tbsp. Thai fish sauce

4 small eggs
salt and pepper
2 tbsp. chopped fresh cilantro, to
    garnish

1 Heat the oil in a large pan or wok. Add the garlic and pork gently for about 1 minute until the meat is broken up but not browned.

2 Stir in the scallions, ginger, chili, and stock, stirring until boiling. Add the rice, lower the heat and simmer for 2 minutes.

3 Add the fish sauce and adjust the seasoning with salt and pepper to taste. Carefully break the eggs into the soup and simmer over a very low heat for 3–4 minutes until set.

4 Ladle the soup into large bowls, allowing 1 egg per portion. Garnish with chopped cilantro and serve.

COOK'S TIP
If you prefer, beat the eggs together and fry like an omelette until set, then cut into ribbon-like strips and added to the soup just before serving.

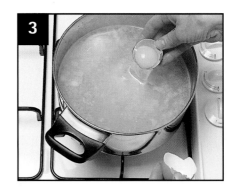

Spinach & Ginger Soup

This mildly spiced, rich green soup is delicately scented with ginger and lemon grass.
It makes a good light appetizer or summer lunch dish.

Serves 4

INGREDIENTS

2 tbsp. sunflower oil
1 onion, chopped
2 garlic cloves, finely chopped
1 inch piece ginger, finely chopped
9 oz. (about 4 cups) fresh young
   spinach leaves

1 small lemon grass stalk, finely
   chopped
4 cups chicken or vegetable stock
1 small potato, peeled and chopped
1 tbsp. rice wine or dry sherry
1 tsp. sesame oil

salt and pepper

1 Heat the oil in a large saucepan. Add the onion, garlic, and ginger and fry gently for 3–4 minutes until softened but not browned.

2 Reserve 2–3 small spinach leaves, then add the remaining leaves and lemon grass to the pan, stirring until the spinach is wilted. Add the stock and potato and bring to a boil. Lower the heat, cover and simmer for about 10 minutes.

3 Tip the soup into a blender or food processor and process until completely smooth.

4 Return the soup to the pan and add the rice wine, then adjust the seasoning to taste with salt and pepper to taste. Heat until almost boiling.

5 Finely shred the reserved spinach leaves and scatter over the top. Drizzle with a few drops of sesame oil and serve hot.

COOK'S TIP

To make a creamy-textured spinach and coconut soup, stir in about 4 tablespoons creamed coconut, or alternatively replace about 1¼ cups of the stock with coconut milk. Serve the soup with shavings of fresh coconut scattered over the surface.

Chilled Avocado, Lime, & Cilantro Soup

*A delightfully simple soup with a blend of typical Thai flavors,
which needs no cooking and can be served at any time of day.*

Serves 4

INGREDIENTS

2 ripe avocados
1 small mild onion, chopped
1 garlic clove, crushed
2 tbsp. chopped fresh cilantro
1 tbsp. chopped fresh mint

2 tbsp. lime juice
scant 3 cups vegetable stock
1 tbsp. rice vinegar
1 tbsp. light soy sauce
salt and pepper

GARNISH:
2 tbsp. sour cream or crème fraiche
1 tbsp. finely chopped cilantro
2 tsp. lime juice
fine shreds of lime rind

1 Halve, pit, and scoop out the flesh from the avocados. Place in a blender or food processor with the onion, garlic, cilantro, mint, lime juice, and about half the stock and process until completely smooth.

2 Add the remaining stock, rice wine vinegar, and soy sauce and blend again to mix well. Taste and adjust seasoning if necessary

with salt and pepper, or with a little extra lime juice if necessary. Cover and chill in the refrigerator until needed.

3 To make the lime and cilantro cream garnish, mix together the sour cream, cilantro, and lime juice. Spoon into the soup just before serving and sprinkle with lime rind.

COOK'S TIP
The top surface of the soup may darken slightly if the soup is stored for longer than about an hour, but don't worry—just give it a quick stir before serving. To reduce the chances of this happening if you plan to keep the soup for several hours, cover it with plastic wrap to seal it from the air.

Meat Fish & Main Dishes

The Thais are primarily a fish-eating nation, and meat takes a back seat in most meals, except for special celebrations. The waterways of Thailand are teeming with many types of fish—even in the channels between the rice paddy fields, and the warm seas bring an abundance of fish and shellfish. So it's hardly surprising that along with rice, fish has long been a vital part of the Thai diet.

Even in the heart of Bangkok city, the markets are teeming with fresh fish and seafood of all kinds. In Thai coastal towns, rows of thatch-roofed beach kiosks purvey every type of fresh seafood from the warm Gulf waters, from barbecued or sautéed fish with ginger, shrimp in coconut milk, and cilantro, or steamed crab, to locals and visitors alike.

Because of the Thai Buddhist religion, which forbids the killing of animals, most butchers in Thailand are immigrant workers, such as Chinese. Religion does not forbid eating meat, though it is often regarded as a special treat. Chicken is much more common than beef, and it's not unusual to see chicken, or sometimes pork, combined with seafood such as shrimp or crab meat—a combination which works surprisingly well. Duck, another Thai favorite, is frequently barbecue-roasted with warm spices and soy or sweet glazes, much as in the Chinese style.

Stir-fried Beef with Bean Sprouts

A quick-and-easy stir-fry for any day of the week, this simple beef recipe is a good one-pan main dish. Serve a simple green side salad to complete the meal.

Serves 4

INGREDIENTS

1 bunch scallions
2 tbsp. sunflower oil
1 garlic clove, crushed
1 tsp. finely chopped fresh ginger
1 lb. 2 oz. tender beef, cut into thin
   strips
1 large red bell pepper, deseeded and

sliced
1 small red chili, deseeded and
   chopped
3 cups fresh bean sprouts
1 small lemon grass stalk, finely
   chopped
2 tbsp. smooth peanut butter

4 tbsp. coconut milk
1 tbsp. rice wine vinegar
1 tbsp. soy sauce
1 tsp. soft light brown sugar
9 oz. medium egg noodles
salt and pepper

1 Trim and thinly slice the scallions, setting aside some slices to use as a garnish.

2 Heat the oil in a wok over a high heat. Add the onions, garlic and ginger and stir-fry for 2–3 minutes to soften. Add the beef and continue stir-frying for 4–5 minutes until browned evenly.

3 Add the bell pepper and stir-fry for an additional 3–4 minutes. Add the chili and bean sprouts and stir-fry for 2 minutes. Mix together the lemon grass, peanut butter, coconut milk, vinegar, soy sauce, and sugar, then stir into the wok.

4 Meanwhile, cook the egg noodles in boiling, lightly salted water for 4 minutes, or

according to the package directions. Drain and stir into the wok, tossing to mix evenly.

5 Adjust seasoning with salt and pepper to taste. Sprinkle with the reserved scallions and serve hot.

Beef Satay with Peanut Sauce

Satay recipes vary throughout the East, but these little beef skewers are a classic version of the traditional dish. The deliciously morish peanut sauce turns the skewers into a rich, substantial dish.

Serves 4

INGREDIENTS

1 lb. 2 oz. beef fillet (tenderloin)
2 garlic cloves, crushed
3/4 inch piece fresh ginger, finely grated
1 tbsp. soft light brown sugar
1 tbsp. dark soy sauce

1 tbsp. lime juice
2 tsp. sesame oil
1 tsp. ground coriander
1 tsp. turmeric
1/2 tsp. chili powder
crisp salad, to serve

PEANUT SAUCE:
8 tbsp. crunchy peanut butter
1/2 small onion, grated
1 1/4 cups coconut milk
2 tsp. soft light brown sugar
1/2 tsp. chili powder
1 tbsp. dark soy sauce

1 Cut the beef into 1/2 inch cubes and place in a large bowl.

2 Add the garlic, ginger, sugar, soy sauce, lime juice, sesame oil, ground coriander, turmeric, and chili powder. Mix well to coat the pieces of meat evenly. Cover and leave to marinate in the refrigerator for at least 2 hours, or overnight.

3 To make the peanut sauce, place all the ingredients in a saucepan and stir over a medium heat until boiling. Remove from the heat and keep warm.

4 Thread the beef cubes on to bamboo skewers. Broil the skewers under a preheated broiler for 3–5 minutes, turning often, until golden. Alternatively, barbecue over hot coals. Serve with the sauce and a crisp salad.

COOK'S TIP

The secret of success for this recipe is to cook the tender cubes of beef very quickly with a high heat, sealing in and retaining all the juices and flavor. Make sure the broiler or grill is very hot before you start to cook. Soak the skewers in cold water for about 20 minutes before threading the meat on to them—this reduces the risk of the skewers burning.

Beef & Peppers with Lemon Grass

A delicately flavored stir-fry infused with lemon grass and ginger.
Colorful peppers help to complete the dish, and it's all cooked within minutes!

Serves 4

INGREDIENTS

1 lb. 2 oz. lean beef fillet (tenderloin)
2 tbsp. vegetable oil
1 garlic clove, finely chopped
1 lemon grass stalk, finely shredded
1 inch piece fresh ginger, finely
   chopped

1 red bell pepper, deseeded and
   thickly sliced
1 green bell pepper, deseeded and
   thickly sliced
1 onion, thickly sliced
2 tbsp. lime juice

boiled noodles or rice, to serve

1 Cut the beef into long, thin strips, cutting across the grain.

2 Heat the oil in a wok or large frying pan over a high heat. Add the garlic and stir-fry for 1 minute. Add the beef and stir-fry for an additional 2–3 minutes until lightly colored. Stir in the lemon grass and ginger and remove the wok from the heat.

3 Remove the beef from the wok or pan and keep to one side. Add the bell peppers and onion to the wok and stir-fry over a high heat for 2–3 minutes until just turning golden brown and slightly softened.

4 Return the beef to the pan, stir in the lime juice and season to taste with salt and pepper. Serve with noodles or rice.

COOK'S TIP

When preparing lemon grass, take care to remove the outer layers that can be tough and fibrous. Use only the center, tender part, which has the finest flavor.

Red-Hot Beef with Cashews

Very hot and spicy, these quick-cooked beef strips are quite filling.
Serve them with lots of plain rice and a cucumber salad to offset the heat.

Serves 4

INGREDIENTS

1 lb. 2 oz. boneless, lean beef sirloin,
    thinly sliced
1 tsp. vegetable oil

MARINADE:
1 tbsp. sesame seeds
1 garlic clove, chopped
1 tbsp. finely chopped fresh ginger
1 red bird's eye chili, chopped
2 tbsp. dark soy sauce
1 tsp. red curry paste

TO FINISH:
1 tsp. sesame oil
4 tbsp. unsalted cashew nuts
1 scallion, thickly sliced diagonally

1 Cut the beef into ½ inch wide strips. Place them in a large, nonmetallic bowl.

2 To make the marinade, toast the sesame seeds in a heavy-based pan over a medium heat for 2–3 minutes until golden brown, shaking the pan occasionally.

3 Place the seeds in a mortar and pestle with the garlic, ginger, and chili and grind to a

smooth paste. Add the soy sauce and curry paste and mix well.

4 Spoon the paste over the beef strips and toss well to coat the meat evenly. Cover and leave to marinate in the refrigertor for 2–3 hours, or overnight.

5 Heat a large griddle or heavy frying pan until very hot and brush with vegetable oil. Place the beef strips over this and cook

quickly, turning often, until lightly browned. Remove from the heat and spoon into a pile on a hot serving dish.

6 Heat the sesame oil in a small pan and quickly fry the cashew nuts until golden. Add the scallions and stir-fry for 30 seconds. Sprinkle on top of the beef strips and serve immediately.

Hot Beef & Coconut Curry

The heat of the chilies in this red-hot curry is balanced and softened by the coconut milk, producing a creamy-textured, rich and lavishly spiced dish.

Serves 4

INGREDIENTS

1³⁄₄ cups coconut milk
2 tbsp. red curry paste
2 garlic cloves, crushed
1lb. 2 oz. braising steak
2 kaffir lime leaves, shredded

3 tbsp. kaffir lime juice
2 tbsp. Thai fish sauce
1 large red chili, deseeded and sliced
½ tsp. turmeric
½ tsp. salt

2 tbsp. chopped fresh basil leaves
2 tbsp. chopped fresh cilantro leaves
shredded coconut, to garnish
boiled rice, to serve

1 Place the coconut milk in a large pan and bring to a boil. Lower the heat and simmer gently over a low heat for about 10 minutes until thickened. Stir in the red curry paste and garlic and simmer for an additional 5 minutes.

2 Cut the beef into ³⁄₄ inch chunks, add to the pan, and bring to a boil, stirring. Lower the heat and add the lime leaves, lime juice, fish sauce, chili, turmeric, and salt.

3 Cover and continue simmering for 20–25 minutes until the meat is tender, adding a little water if the sauce looks too dry.

4 Stir in the basil and cilantro and adjust the seasoning with salt and pepper to taste. Sprinkle with coconut and serve with boiled rice.

COOK'S TIP

This recipe uses one of the larger, milder red chili peppers—either fresno or Dutch—simply because they give more color to the dish. If you prefer to use small Thai, or bird's eye, chilies, you'll still need only one as they are much hotter.

Roasted Red Pork

*This red-glazed, sweet-and-tender pork, of Chinese origin, is a colorful addition
to many stir-fries, salads and soups. Or simply serve it sliced and arranged
on a wide platter over a bed of Chinese cabbage.*

Serves 4

INGREDIENTS

1 lb. 5 oz. pork tenderloins
shredded Chinese cabbage, to serve

MARINADE:
2 garlic cloves, crushed
1 tbsp. grated fresh ginger

1 tbsp. light soy sauce
1 tbsp. Thai fish sauce
1 tbsp. rice wine
1 tbsp. hoisin sauce
1 tbsp. sesame oil
1 tbsp. palm sugar or brown sugar

½ tsp. five-spice powder
a few drops red food coloring
(optional)

1 Mix together all the ingredients for the marinade and spread over the pork, turning to coat evenly. Place in a large dish, cover, and leave to marinate in the refrigerator overnight.

2 Place a rack in a roasting pan, then half-fill the pan with boiling water. Lift the pork from the marinade and place it on the rack. Reserve the marinade.

3 Roast in a preheated oven at 425° F for about 20 minutes. Baste with the marinade, then lower the heat to 350° F and continue roasting for an additional 35-40 minutes, basting occasionally with the marinade, until the pork is a rich reddish brown and thoroughly cooked.

4 Cut the pork into thick slices and serve on a bed of shredded Chinese cabbage.

COOK'S TIP

The pork may also be cooked by broiling. Simply cut the meat into slices or strips and coat in the marinade , then arrange on a foil-lined broiler pan and broil under a high heat, turning occasionally and basting with marinade.

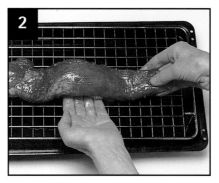

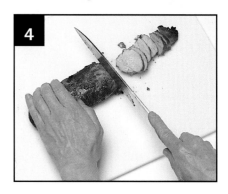

Pork with Soy & Sesame Glaze

Thai cooks are fond of adding sweet flavors to meat, as in this unusual pork dish, with soy and garlic to balance the sweetness of the honey. Pork tenderloin is a very lean meat, so take care not to overcook or it will be dry.

Serves 4

INGREDIENTS

2 pork tenderloins, about 10 oz. each
2 tbsp. dark soy sauce
2 tbsp. honey
2 garlic cloves, crushed

1 tbsp. sesame seeds
1 onion, thinly sliced in rings
1 tbsp. seasoned all-purpose flour
sunflower oil for frying

crisp salad, to serve

1 Trim the pork tenderloins and place them in a wide nonmetallic dish.

2 Mix together the soy, honey, and garlic. Spread this mixture over the pork, turning the meat to coat it evenly.

3 Lift the pork tenderloins into a roasting pan or shallow ovenproof dish. Sprinkle evenly with sesame seeds.

4 Roast the pork in an oven preheated at 400° F for about 20 minutes, spooning over any juices. Cover loosely with foil to prevent over-browning and roast for an additional 10-15 minutes until thoroughly cooked.

5 Meanwhile, dip the onion slices in the flour and shake off the excess. Heat the oil and fry the onion rings until golden and crisp, turning occasionally. Serve the pork in slices with the crisply fried onions on a bed of crisp salad.

COOK'S TIP

This pork is also excellent served cold, and it's a good choice for picnics, especially served with a spicy sambal or chili relish.

Stir-fried Pork and Corn

A speedy dish, typical of Thai street food. This includes fresh corn, which,
although introduced relatively recently to Thailand, is a very popular vegetable used in many dishes.
Fresh corn-on-the-cob, the fresher the better, is first choice, but if it's not available,
use drained, canned corn instead.

Serves 4

INGREDIENTS

2 tbsp. vegetable oil
1 lb. 2 oz. lean boneless pork, cut in
thin strips
1 garlic clove, chopped
2 cups fresh corn kernels

1½ cups green beans, cut into short
lengths
2 scallions, chopped
1 small red chili, chopped
1 tsp. sugar

1 tbsp. light soy sauce
3 tbsp. chopped fresh cilantro
egg noodles or boiled rice, to serve

1 Heat the oil in a wok and stir-fry the pork quickly over a high heat until lightly browned.

2 Stir in the garlic, corn, beans, scallions, and chili and continue stir-frying for 2–3 minutes.

3 Stir in the sugar and soy sauce stir-fry for 30 seconds.

4 Sprinkle with the cilantro and serve immediately with egg noodles or rice.

COOK'S TIP

In Thailand, "long beans" would be used for dishes such as this, but we have substituted green beans, which are more easily available. But look out for long beans in Asian food stores—they are like long string beans and have a similar flavor, but their texture is crisp, and they cook more quickly.

Spicy Fried Minced Pork

A warmly spiced dish, this is ideal for a quick family meal. Just cook fine egg noodles for an accompaniment while the meat sizzles, and dinner can be on the table in a matter of minutes!

Serves 4

INGREDIENTS

2 garlic cloves
3 shallots
1 inch piece fresh ginger
2 tbsp. sunflower oil
1 lb. 2 oz. lean ground pork

2 tbsp. Thai fish sauce
1 tbsp. dark soy sauce
1 tbsp. red curry paste
4 dried kaffir lime leaves, crumbled
4 plum tomatoes, chopped

3 tbsp. chopped fresh cilantro
salt and pepper
boiled fine egg noodles, to serve

1 Peel and finely chop the garlic, shallots and ginger. Heat the oil in a wok over a medium heat. Add the garlic, shallots and ginger and stir-fry for about 2 minutes. Stir in the pork and continue stir-frying until golden brown.

2 Stir in the fish sauce, soy sauce, curry paste and lime leaves, and stir-fry for a further 1–2 minutes over a high heat.

3 Add the tomatoes and cook for a further 5–6 minutes, stirring occasionally.

4 Stir in the chopped cilantro and season to taste with salt and pepper. Serve hot, spooned on to boiled fine egg noodles, garnished with coriander sprigs.

COOK'S TIP

Dried kaffir lime leaves are a useful storecupboard (pantry) ingredient as they can be crumbled easily straight into quick dishes such as this. If you prefer to use fresh kaffir lime leaves, shred them finely and add to the dish.

Thai-spiced Sausages

These mildly spiced little sausages are a good choice for a buffet meal.
They can be made a day in advance, and are equally good served hot or cold.

Serves 4

INGREDIENTS

14 oz. lean ground pork

4 tbsp. cooked rice

1 garlic clove, crushed

1 tsp. red curry paste

1 tsp. ground black pepper

1 tsp. ground coriander

½ tsp. salt

3 tbsp. lime juice

2 tbsp. chopped fresh cilantro

3 tbsp. peanut oil

coconut sambal or soy sauce, to serve

1 Place the pork, rice, garlic, curry paste, pepper, ground coriander, salt, lime juice, and chopped cilantro in a bowl and knead together with your hands to mix evenly.

2 Use your hands to shape the mixture into 12 small sausage shapes. If you can buy sausage casings, fill the casings and twist at intervals to separate the sausages.

3 Heat the oil in a large frying pan over a medium heat. Add the sausages and fry for 8-10 minutes, turning them over occasionally, until they are evenly golden brown. Serve hot with a coconut sambal or soy sauce.

COOK'S TIP

These sausages can also be served as an appetizer—shape the mixture slightly smaller to make about 16 bite-sized sausages. Serve with a soy dip.

Thai-style Burgers

If your family like to eat burgers, try these—they have a much more interesting flavor than conventional hamburgers!

Serves 4

INGREDIENTS

1 small lemon grass stalk
1 small red chili, deseeded
2 garlic cloves, peeled
2 scallions
2½ cups button mushrooms
14 oz. ground pork

1 tbsp. Thai fish sauce
3 tbsp. chopped fresh cilantro
sunflower oil for pan-frying
2 tbsp. mayonnaise
1 tbsp. lime juice
salt and pepper

TO SERVE:
4 sesame hamburger buns
shredded Chinese cabbage

1 Place the lemon grass, chili, garlic, and scallions in a food processor and process to a smooth paste. Add the mushrooms and process until very finely chopped.

2 Add the ground pork, fish sauce, and cilantro, then season well with salt and pepper. Divide the mixture into 4 equal portions and shape with lightly floured hands into flat burger shapes.

3 Heat the oil in a wide frying pan over a medium heat. Add the burgers and fry for 6–8 minutes until done as you like.

4 Meanwhile, mix the mayonnaise with the lime juice. Split the hamburger buns and spread the lime-flavored mayonnaise on the cut surfaces. Add a few shredded Chinese cabbage, top with a burger and sandwich together. Serve immediately.

COOK'S TIP

You can add a spoonful of your favorite relish to each burger, or alternatively, add a few pieces of crisp pickled vegetables for a change of texture (see page 160).

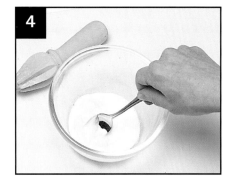

Red Lamb Curry

*This richly spiced curry uses the typically red-hot chili flavor of Thai red curry paste,
made with dried red chilies, to give it a warm, russet-red color.*

Serves 4

INGREDIENTS

1 lb. 2 oz. boneless lean leg of lamb
2 tbsp. vegetable oil
1 large onion, sliced
2 garlic cloves, crushed
2 tbsp. Thai red curry paste
²/₃ cup coconut milk

1 tbsp. soft light brown sugar
1 large red bell pepper, deseeded and
   thickly sliced
½ cup beef (or lamb) stock
1 tbsp. Thai fish sauce
2 tbsp. lime juice

8 oz. can water chestnuts, drained
2 tbsp. chopped fresh cilantro
2 tbsp. chopped fresh basil
salt and pepper
boiled jasmine rice, to serve

1 Trim the meat and cut it into 1¼ inch cubes. Heat the oil in a wok over a high heat and stir-fry the onion and garlic for 2–3 minutes to soften. Add the meat cubes and fry quickly until lightly browned.

2 Stir in the curry paste and cook for a few seconds, then add the coconut milk and sugar and bring to a boil. Reduce the heat and simmer for 15 minutes, stirring occasionally.

3 Stir in the red bell pepper, stock, fish sauce and lime juice, cover and continue simmering for an additional 15 minutes, or until the meat is tender.

4 Add the water chestnuts, cilantro and basil, then adjust the seasoning to taste. Serve with jasmine rice.

COOK'S TIP

This curry can also be made with other lean red meats. Try replacing the lamb with trimmed duck breasts or pieces of lean braising beef.

Roast Chicken with Ginger & Lime

This is a version of a sweet-and-sour chicken dish often sold by street traders in the East –
they barbecue the chickens either whole or cut in half, then chop it into pieces to sell.
Begin the preparation the day before you cook , or at least early in the day,
to give the flavors plenty of time to penetrate the chicken.

Serves 4

INGREDIENTS

1¼ inch piece fresh ginger, finely chopped	½ tsp. salt	2 tbsp. honey
2 garlic cloves, finely chopped	1 tsp. black peppercorns	1 tsp. cornstarch
1 small onion, finely chopped	3 lb. 5 oz. roasting chicken	2 tsp. water
1 lemon grass stalk, finely chopped	1 tbsp. coconut cream	
	2 tbsp. lime juice	

1 Put the ginger, garlic, onion, lemon grass, salt, and peppercorns in a mortar and pestle and crush to form a smooth paste.

2 Cut the chicken in half lengthways, using poultry shears or strong kitchen scissors. Spread the paste all over the chicken, both inside and out, and spread it directly on to the flesh under the breast skin. Cover and refrigerate overnight, or at least several hours.

3 In a small pan, heat the coconut cream, lime juice, and honey together, stirring until smooth. Brush a little of the mixture evenly over the chicken.

4 Place the chicken halves on a tray over a roasting pan half-filled with boiling water. Roast in an oven preheated to 350° F for about 1 hour, or until the chicken is a rich golden brown, basting occasionally with the reserved lime and honey mixture.

5 When the chicken is cooked, boil the water from the roasting pan to reduce it to about a scant ½ cup. Blend the cornstarch with the water and stir into the reduced liquid. Heat gently until boiling, then stir until slightly thickened and clear. Serve the chicken with the sauce spooned over and a selection of stir-fried vegetables.

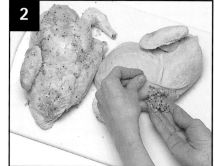

Chicken & Mango Stir-fry

A colorful, exotic mix of flavors that works surprisingly well,
this dish is easy and quick to cook—ideal for a midweek family meal.

Serves 4

INGREDIENTS

6 boneless, skinless chicken thighs
1 inch piece fresh ginger, grated
1 garlic clove, crushed
1 small red chili, deseeded
1 large red bell pepper
4 scallions

1½ cups snow peas
1 cup baby corn
1 large firm, ripe mango
2 tbsp. sunflower oil
1 tbsp. light soy sauce
3 tbsp. rice wine or sherry

1 tsp. sesame oil
salt and pepper

1 Cut the chicken into long, thin strips and place in a bowl. Mix together the ginger, garlic, and chili, then stir into the chicken strips to coat them evenly.

2 Slice the bell pepper thinly, cutting diagonally. Trim and diagonally slice the scallions. Cut the snow peas and corn in half diagonally. Peel the mango, remove the pit, and slice thinly.

3 Heat the oil in a wok or large frying pan over a high heat. Add the chicken and stir-fry for 4–5 minutes until just turning golden brown. Add the bell peppers and stir-fry over a medium heat for 4–5 minutes to soften.

4 Add the scallions, corn, and snow peas and stir-fry for an additional minute.

5 Mix together the soy sauce, rice wine or sherry and sesame oil and stir it into the wok. Add the mango and stir gently for 1 minute to heat thoroughly. Adjust the seasoning with salt and pepper to taste and serve immediately.

Thai-Spiced Cilantro Chicken

These simple marinated chicken breasts are packed with powerful, zesty flavors,
and are best accompanied by simple dish of plain boiled rice and a cucumber salad.

Serves 4

INGREDIENTS

4 boneless chicken breasts, without skin

2 garlic cloves, peeled

1 fresh green chili, deseeded

$3/4$ in. piece fresh ginger, peeled

4 tbsp. chopped fresh cilantro

finely grated rind of 1 lime

3 tbsp. lime juice

2 tbsp. light soy sauce

1 tbsp. superfine sugar

$3/4$ cup coconut milk

1 Using a sharp knife, cut 3 deep slashes into the skinned side of each chicken breast. Place the breasts in a single layer in a wide, nonmetallic dish.

2 Put the garlic, chili, ginger, cilantro, lime rind, and juice, soy sauce, superfine sugar and coconut milk in a food processor and process until a smooth puree forms.

3 Spread the puree over both sides of the chicken breasts, coating them evenly. Cover the dish and leave to marinate in the refrigerator for about 1 hour.

4 Lift the chicken from the marinade, drain off the excess, and place on a baking sheet. Broil under a preheated broiler for 12-15 minutes until thoroughly and evenly cooked.

5 Meanwhile, place the remaining marinade in a saucepan and bring to a boil. Lower the heat and simmer for several minutes to heat thoroughly. Serve with the chicken breasts.

Green Chicken Curry

Thai curries are traditionally very hot, and designed to make a little go a long way—the thin, highly spiced juices are eaten with lots of rice to "stretch" a small amount of meat as far as possible.

Serves 4

INGREDIENTS

6 boneless, skinless chicken thighs
1³/₄ cups coconut milk
2 garlic cloves, crushed
2 tbsp. Thai fish sauce

2 tbsp. green curry paste
12 baby eggplants
3 green chilies, finely chopped
3 kaffir lime leaves, shredded

4 tbsp. chopped fresh cilantro
boiled rice, to serve

1 Cut the chicken into bite-sized pieces. Pour the coconut milk into a wok or large pan over a high heat and bring to a boil.

2 Add the chicken, garlic, and fish sauce to the pan and bring back to a boil. Lower the heat and simmer gently for 30 minutes, or until the chicken is tender.

3 Remove the chicken from the mixture with a slotted spoon and set aside and keep warm.

4 Stir the green curry paste into the pan, then add the eggplant, chilies, and lime leaves and simmer for 5 minutes.

5 Return the chicken to the pan and bring to a boil. Adjust the seasoning to taste with salt and pepper, then stir in the cilantro. Serve the curry with plain rice.

COOK'S TIP

Baby eggplants, also called "Thai apple" or "Thai pea" eggplants, are traditionally used in this curry, but they are not always easily available outside the country. If you can't find them in an Asian food shop, use Japanese eggplant (a mild, slender variety) chopped small.

Braised Chicken with Garlic & Spices

The intense flavors of this dish are helped by the slow, gentle cooking. The meat should be almost falling off the bone, virtually "melting" into the velvety-smooth, spicy sauce.

Serves 4

INGREDIENTS

4 garlic cloves, chopped

4 shallots, chopped

2 small red chilies, deseeded and chopped

1 lemon grass stalk, finely chopped

1 tbsp. chopped fresh cilantro

1 tsp. shrimp paste

½ tsp. ground cinnamon

1 tbsp. tamarind paste

2 tbsp. vegetable oil

8 small chicken drumsticks or thighs

1¼ cups chicken stock

1 tbsp. Thai fish sauce

1 tbsp. smooth peanut butter

salt and pepper

4 tbsp. chopped toasted peanuts

1 Place the garlic, shallots, chilies, lemon grass, cilantro, and shrimp paste in a mortar and pestle and grind to an almost smooth paste. Add the cinnamon and tamarind paste.

2 Heat the oil in a wok or wide frying pan. Add the chicken drumsticks, turning often, until they are golden brown on all sides. Remove them from the wok and keep hot. Pour off any excess fat.

3 Add the spice paste to the wok or pan and stir over a medium heat until lightly browned. Stir in the stock and return the chicken to the wok.

4 Bring to a boil, then cover tightly, lower the heat and simmer for 25–30 minutes, stirring occasionally, until the chicken is tender and thoroughly cooked. Stir in the fish sauce and peanut butter and simmer gently for an additional 10 minutes.

5 Adjust the seasoning with salt and pepper to taste and scatter the toasted peanuts over. Serve hot, with colorful stir-fry vegetables and noodles.

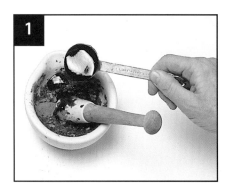

Duck Breasts with Chili & Lime

Duck is excellent cooked with strong flavors, and when it is marinated and coated in this rich, dark, sticky Asian glaze it's irresistible. Serve with jasmine rice and a salad.

Serves 4

INGREDIENTS

4 boneless duck breasts	1 tbsp. soy sauce	2 tbsp. plum jam
2 garlic cloves, crushed	1 tsp. chili sauce	½ cup chicken stock
4 tsp. light soft brown sugar	1 tsp. vegetable oil	salt and pepper
3 tbsp. lime juice		

1 Using a small sharp knife, cut deep slashes in the skin of the duck to make a diamond pattern. Place the duck breasts in a wide, nonmetallic dish.

2 Mix together the garlic, sugar, lime juice, and soy and chili sauces, then spoon over the duck breasts, turning well to coat them evenly. Cover the dish with plastic wrap and leave to marinate in the refrigerator for at least 3 hours, or overnight.

3 Drain the duck, reserving the marinade. Heat a large, heavy-based pan until very hot and brush with the oil. Add the duck breasts, skin side down, and cook for 4–5 minutes until the skin is browned and crisp. Pour off the excess fat.

4 Turn the duck breasts and cook on the other side for 2–3 minutes to brown. Add the reserved marinade, plum jam, and stock and simmer for 2 minutes. Adjust the seasoning to taste and serve hot, with the juices spooned over.

COOK'S TIP

If you prefer to reduce the overall fat content of this dish, remove the skin from the duck breasts before cooking, and reduce the cooking time slightly.

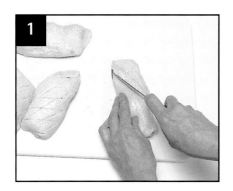

Roasted Duck Curried with Pineapple & Coconut

Duck is a fatty meat, but it has lots of rich flavor. In this recipe, the duck is 'roasted' under a hot broiler until golden brown and crispy, so much of the fat drains off before adding the meat to the curry.

Serves 4

INGREDIENTS

3½ lb. duckling
2 tbsp. peanut oil
1 small pineapple
1 large onion, chopped
1 garlic clove, finely chopped

1 tsp. finely chopped fresh ginger
½ tsp. ground coriander
1 tbsp. green Thai curry paste
1 tsp. soft light brown sugar
2 cups coconut milk

salt and pepper
chopped fresh cilantro, to garnish
boiled jasmine rice, to serve

1 Using a large sharp knife or poultry shears, cut the duck in half lengthways, cutting through the line of the breastbone. Wipe the duckling inside and out with paper towels. Sprinkle with salt and pepper, prick the skin all over with a fork, and brush lightly with oil.

2 Place the duck, cut side down, on a broiler pan and broil under a preheated broiler for 25–30 minutes, turning occasionally, until golden brown. Carefully pour off the fat in the pan, as this may burn.

3 Allow the duck to cool a bit, then cut each half into 2 portions. Peel and core the pineapple, then cut the flesh into small dice.

4 Heat the remaining oil in a large pan and fry the onion and garlic for 3–4 minutes until softened. Stir in the ginger, ground coriander, curry paste, and brown sugar and stir-fry for 1 minute.

5 Stir in the coconut milk and bring to a boil. Add the duck and the pineapple. Reduce the heat and simmer for 5 minutes. Serve over boiled jasmine rice.

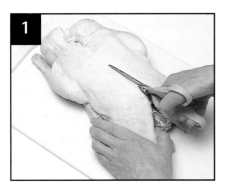

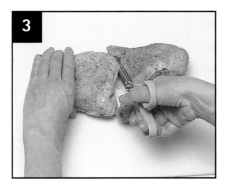

Steamed Yellow Fish Fillets

Thailand has an abundance of fresh fish, and fish is an important part of the local diet. Dishes such as these steamed fillets are popular, and can be adapted to suit many different types of fish, depending on what's available.

Serves 4

INGREDIENTS

1 lb. 2 oz. firm fish fillets, such as red snapper, sole, or monkfish
1 dried red bird's eye chili
1 small onion, chopped
3 garlic cloves, chopped

2 sprigs fresh cilantro
1 tsp. coriander seeds
½ tsp. turmeric
½ tsp. ground black pepper
1 tbsp. Thai fish sauce

2 tbsp. coconut milk
1 small egg, beaten
2 tbsp. rice flour
soy sauce, to serve

1 Remove any skin from the fish and cut the fillets diagonally into long ¾ inch wide strips.

2 Place the dried chili, onion, garlic, cilantro, and coriander seeds in a mortar and pestle and grind to a smooth paste.

3 Add the turmeric, pepper, fish sauce, coconut milk, and beaten egg, stirring well to mix evenly.

4 Dip the fish strips into the paste mixture, then into the rice flour to coat lightly.

5 Bring the water in the bottom of a steamer to a boil, then arrange the fish strips in the top of the steamer. Cover and steam for 12–15 minutes until the fish is just firm.

6 Serve the fish with soy sauce and an accompaniment of stir-fried vegetables or salad.

COOK'S TIP

If you don't have a steamer, improvise by placing a large metal colander over a large pan of boiling water and cover with an upturned plate to enclose the fish as it steams.

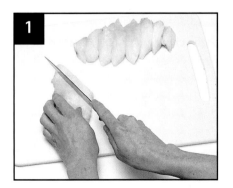

Baked Fish with Peppers, Chili & Basil

Almost any whole fish can be cooked by this method, but snapper, sea bass or
John Dory are particularly good with the Thai flavors.

Serves 4

INGREDIENTS

handful of fresh sweet basil leaves
1 lb. 10 oz. whole red snapper, sea
   bass, or John Dory, cleaned
2 tbsp. peanut oil
2 tbsp. Thai fish sauce
2 garlic cloves, crushed

1 tsp. finely grated galangal or ginger
2 large fresh red chilies, sliced
   diagonally
1 yellow bell pepper, deseeded and
   diced
1 tbsp. palm sugar (or brown sugar)

1 tbsp. rice vinegar
2 tbsp. water or fish stock
2 tomatoes, deseeded and sliced into
   thin wedges

1 Reserve a few fresh basil leaves for garnish and tuck the rest inside the body cavity of the fish.

2 Heat 1 tablespoon oil in a wide frying pan and fry the fish quickly to brown, turning once. Place the fish on a large piece of foil in a roasting pan and spoon over the fish sauce. Wrap the foil over loosely and bake in an oven preheated to 375° F for 25–30 minutes until just cooked though.

3 Meanwhile, heat the remaining oil and fry the garlic, galangal and chili for 30 seconds. Add the peppers and stir-fry for an additional 2–3 minutes to soften.

4 Stir in the sugar, rice vinegar, and water, then add the tomatoes and bring to a boil. Remove the pan from the heat.

5 Remove the fish from the oven and transfer to a warmed serving plate. Add the fish juices to the pan, then spoon the sauce over the fish and scatter with the reserved basil leaves. Serve immediately.

COOK'S TIP

Large red chilies are less hot than the tiny bird's eye chilies, so you can use them more freely in cooked dishes such as this for a mild heat. Remove the seeds if you prefer.

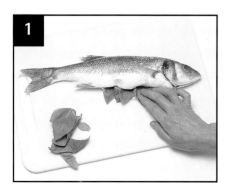

Baked Cod with a Curry Crust

An easy, economical main dish that transforms a plain piece of fish into an exotic meal—try it with other white fish, too, such as monkfish or halibut. Serve this with new potatoes and salad.

Serves 4

INGREDIENTS

½ tsp. sesame oil
4 pieces cod fillet, about 150 g/5½ oz. each
80 g/3 oz/1½ cups fresh white breadcrumbs

2 tbsp. chopped blanched almonds
2 tsp. green Thai curry paste
finely grated rind of ½ lime
salt and pepper

TO GARNISH:
lime slices
cilantro sprigs

1 Brush the sesame oil over the base of a wide, shallow oven-proof dish or pan, then place the pieces of cod in a single layer.

2 Mix together the breadcrumbs, almonds, curry paste and grated lime rind, stirring well to blend thoroughly and evenly. Season to taste with salt and pepper.

3 Carefully spoon the crumb mixture over the fish pieces, pressing lightly to hold it in place.

4 Place the dish, uncovered, in a preheated oven at 200°C/400° F/Gas Mark 6 and bake for 35-40 minutes until the fish is cooked through and the crumb topping is golden brown. Serve hot.

COOK'S TIP

To test whether the fish is cooked through, use a fork to pierce it in the thickest part-if the flesh is white all the way through and flakes apart easily it is cooked sufficiently.

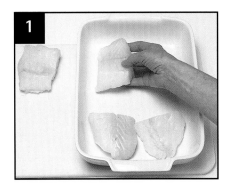

Whole Fried Fish with Soy & Ginger

This impressive dish is worth cooking for a special dinner, as it really is a talking point.
Buy a very fresh whole fish on the day you plan to cook it, and ask your fishmonger to clean it,
preferably leaving the head on.

Serves 4-6

INGREDIENTS

6 dried Chinese mushrooms
3 tbsp. rice vinegar
2 tbsp. soft light brown sugar
3 tbsp. dark soy sauce
3 in. piece fresh ginger, finely
  chopped

4 scallions, sliced diagonally
2 tsp. cornstarch
2 tbsp. lime juice
1 sea bass, about 2 lb. 4 oz, cleaned
salt and pepper
4 tbsp. all-purpose flour

sunflower oil for deep frying

1 Soak the dried mushrooms in hot water for about 10 minutes, then drain well, reserving a scant ½ cup of the liquid. Cut the mushrooms into thin slices.

2 Mix the reserved mushroom liquid with the rice vinegar, sugar, and soy sauce. Place in a saucepan with the mushrooms and bring to a boil. Reduce the heat and simmer for 3–4 minutes.

3 Add the ginger and scallions and simmer for 1 minute. Blend the cornstarch and lime juice together, stir into the pan and stir for 1–2 minutes until the sauce thickens and clears. Keep the sauce to one side while you cook the fish.

4 Season the fish inside and out with salt and pepper, then dust lightly with flour, shaking off the excess.

5 Heat a 1 inch depth of oil in a wide pan to 375° F, or until a cube of bread browns in 40 seconds. Carefully lower the fish into the oil and fry on one side for about 3–4 minutes until golden brown. Use 2 metal spatulas to turn the fish carefully and fry on the other side for an additional 3–4 minutes until golden brown.

6 Lift the fish out of the pan, draining off the excess oil, and place on a serving plate. Heat the sauce until boiling, then spoon it over the fish. Serve immediately.

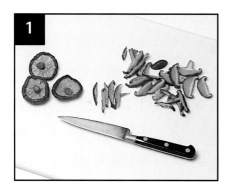

Spiced Tuna in Sweet-sour Sauce

Tuna is a firm, meaty-textured fish that is abundant in the seas around Thailand.
You can also use shark or mackerel with this rich sweet-sour sauce.

Serves 4

INGREDIENTS

4 fresh tuna steaks, about 1 lb. 2 oz.
  total weight
$1/4$ tsp. ground black pepper
2 tbsp. peanut oil
1 onion, diced
1 small red bell pepper, deseeded and
  cut into matchsticks
1 garlic clove, crushed

½ cucumber, deseeded and cut into
  matchsticks
2 pineapple slices, diced
1 tsp. finely chopped fresh ginger
1 tbsp. soft light brown sugar
1 tbsp. cornstarch
1½ tbsp. lime juice
1 tbsp. Thai fish sauce

generous 1 cup fish stock

TO GARNISH:
lime wedges
cucumber slices

1 Sprinkle the tuna steaks with pepper on both sides. Heat a griddle or heavy frying pan and brush with a little of the oil. Arrange the tuna on the griddle and cook for about 8 minutes, turning them over once.

2 Heat the remaining oil in another pan and fry the onion, pepper, and garlic gently for 3–4 minutes to soften.

3 Remove from the heat and stir in the cucumber, pineapple, ginger, and sugar.

4 Blend the cornstarch with the lime juice and fish sauce, then stir into the stock and add to the pan. Stir over a medium heat until boiling, then cook for 1–2 minutes until thickened and clear.

5 Spoon the sauce over the tuna and serve garnished with lime wedges and cucumber.

COOK'S TIP

Tuna can be served quite slightly cooked, and can be dry if it is overcooked

Thai-spiced Salmon

Marinated in delicate Thai spices and quickly pan-fried to perfection, these salmon fillets are ideal for a special dinner. Serve them fresh from the pan to enjoy them at their best.

Serves 4

INGREDIENTS

1 in. piece fresh root ginger, grated
1 tsp. coriander seeds, crushed
¹/₄ tsp. chili powder

1 tbsp. lime juice
1 tsp. sesame oil

4 pieces salmon fillet with skin , about
5½ oz. each
2 tbsp. vegetable oil

1 Mix together the ginger, coriander, chili, lime juice, and sesame oil.

2 Place the salmon in a wide, nonmetallic plate or dish and spoon the mixture over the flesh side of the fillets, spreading it to coat each piece of salmon evenly.

3 Cover the dish with plastic wrap and chill the salmon in the refrigerator for 30 minutes.

4 Heat a wide, heavy-based frying pan or griddle pan with the oil over a high heat. Place the salmon on the hot pan or griddle, skin side down.

5 Cook the salmon for 4–5 minutes, without turning, until the salmon is crusty underneath and the flesh flakes easily. Serve at once.

COOK'S TIP

It's important to use a heavy-based pan or solid griddle for this recipe, so the fish cooks evenly throughout without sticking. If the fish is very thick, you may prefer to turn it over carefully to cook on the other side for 2–3 minutes.

Salmon with Red Curry in Banana Leaves

Banana leaves are widely used in Thai cooking to wrap raw foods such as fish before baking or steaming. Asian food shops usually stock them, but if you can't find any use foil or baking parchment.

Serves 4

INGREDIENTS

4 salmon steaks, about 6 oz. each
2 banana leaves, halved
1 garlic clove, crushed
1 tsp. grated fresh ginger
1 tbsp. red Thai curry paste

1 tsp. soft light brown sugar
1 tbsp. Thai fish sauce
2 tbsp. lime juice

TO GARNISH:

lime slices
scallion slices

1 Place a salmon steak on the center of each banana leaf half.

2 Mix together the garlic, ginger, curry paste, sugar, and fish sauce. Spread this mixture over the surface of the fish and sprinkle with lime juice.

3 Wrap the banana leaves around the fish, tucking in the sides as you go, to make a neat bundle. Seal with toothpicks.

4 Place the packages seam side down on a baking sheet and bake in a preheated oven at 425° F for 15–20 minutes until the fish is cooked and the banana leaves are beginning to brown.

COOK'S TIP

Fresh banana leaves are often sold in packs containing several leaves, but if you buy more than you need they will store in the refrigerator for about a week.

Spicy Thai Seafood Stew

The fish in this fragrant, curry-like stew can be varied according to taste or availability, but it's best to stick with those which stay firm when cooked, as delicate types will flake apart too easily.

Serves 4

INGREDIENTS

1 lb. 2 oz. firm white fish fillet, preferably monkfish or halibut
7 oz. squid, cleaned
1 tbsp. sunflower oil
4 shallots, finely chopped
2 garlic cloves, finely chopped

2 tbsp. Thai green curry paste
2 small lemon grass stalks, finely chopped
1 tsp. shrimp paste
2¼ cups coconut milk

7 oz. raw peeled jumbo shrimp, deveined
12 fresh clams in shell, cleaned
8 basil leaves, finely shredded
boiled rice, to serve

1 Cut the fish into bite-sized chunks, and cut the squid body cavities into thick rings.

2 Heat the oil in a large frying pan or wok and stir-fry the shallots, garlic, and curry paste for 1–2 minutes. Add the lemon grass and shrimp paste, stir in the coconut milk and bring to a boil.

3 Reduce the heat until the liquid is simmering gently, then add the white fish, squid, and shrimp to the pan and simmer for 2 minutes.

4 Add the clams and simmer for an additional minute until the clams open. Discard any clams that do not open.

5 Scatter the basil leaves over the stew and serve immediately, spooned over boiled rice.

COOK'S TIP

If you prefer, fresh mussels in the shell can be used instead of clams—add them in Step 4 and follow the recipe.

Stir-fried Squid with Hot Black Bean Sauce

Quick stir-frying is an ideal cooking method for squid, as if overcooked it can be tough. It also seals in the natural colors, flavors and nutritive value of fresh vegetables.

Serves 4

INGREDIENTS

1 lb. 10 oz. squid, cleaned
1 large red bell pepper, deseeded
1 cup snow peas, trimmed
1 head bok choi
3 tbsp. black bean sauce
1 tbsp. Thai fish sauce

1 tbsp. rice wine
1 tbsp. dark soy sauce
1 tsp. soft light brown sugar
1 tsp. cornstarch
1 tbsp. water
1 tbsp. sunflower oil

1 tsp. sesame oil
1 small red bird's eye chili, chopped
1 garlic clove, finely chopped
1 tsp. grated fresh ginger
2 scallions, chopped

1 Cut the tentacles from the squid and discard. Cut the body cavities into quarters lengthways. Use the tip of a small sharp knife to score a diamond pattern into the flesh, without cutting all the way through. Pat dry with paper towels.

2 Cut the bell pepper into long, thin slices. Cut the snow peas out in half diagonally. Coarsely shred the bok choi.

3 Mix together the black bean sauce, fish sauce, rice wine, soy sauce, and sugar. Blend the cornstarch with the water and stir into the other ingredients. Keep to one side.

4 Heat the oils in a wok. Add the chili, garlic, ginger, and scallions and stir-fry for about 1 minute. Add the bell pepper and stir-fry for about 2 minutes.

5 Add the squid and stir-fry over a high heat for an additional minute. Stir in the snowpeas and bok choi and stir for an additional minute until wilted.

6 Stir in the sauce ingredients and cook, stirring, for about 2 minutes, until the sauce clears and thickens. Serve immediately.

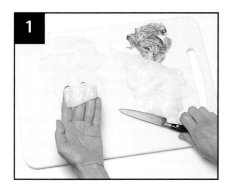

Spicy Scallops with Lime & Chili

Really fresh scallops have a delicate flavor and texture, needing only minimal cooking, as in this simple stir-fry.

Serves 4

INGREDIENTS

16 large scallops
1 tbsp. butter
1 tbsp. vegetable oil
1 tsp. crushed garlic
1 tsp. grated fresh ginger

1 bunch scallions, finely sliced
finely grated rind of 1 kaffir lime
1 small red chili, deseeded and sliced
3 tbsp. kaffir lime juice
salt and pepper

TO SERVE:
lime wedges
boiled rice

1 Trim the scallops to remove any black intestine, then wash and pat dry. Separate the corals from the white parts, then slice each white part in half horizontally, making 2 rounds.

2 Heat the butter and oil in a wok. Add the garlic and ginger and stir-fry for 1 minute, without browning. Add the scallions and stir-fry for 1 more minute.

3 Add the scallops and continue stir-frying over a high heat for 4–5 minutes. Stir in the lime rind, chili, and lime juice and cook for an additional minute.

4 Serve the scallops hot, with juices spooned over, accompanied by lime wedges and boiled rice.

COOK'S TIP

If fresh scallops are not available, frozen ones can be used, but make sure they are thoroughly thawed before you cook them. Drained off all excess moisture and pat dry with paper towels.

Shrimp Skewers with Chili & Tamarind Glaze

*Whole jumbo shrimp cook very quickly on a grill or under a broiler
so they're ideal for summertime cooking, in- or outdoors—all you need is a fresh salad
and the meal is complete.*

Serves 4

INGREDIENTS

1 garlic clove, chopped
1 bird's eye chili, deseeded and
  chopped
1 tbsp. tamarind paste
1 tbsp. sesame oil

1 tbsp. dark soy sauce
2 tbsp. lime juice
1 tbsp. soft light brown sugar
16 large whole raw jumbo shrimp

TO SERVE:
crusty bread
4 lime wedges

1 Place the garlic, chili, tamarind, sesame oil, soy sauce, lime juice, and sugar in a small pan. Stir over a low heat until the sugar is dissolved, then remove from the heat and allow to cool completely.

2 Wash and dry the shrimp and place in a single layer in a wide, nonmetallic dish. Spoon the marinade over the shrimp and turn them over to coat evenly. Cover the dish and leave to marinate in the refrigerator for at least 2 hours, or overnight.

3 Meanwhile, soak 4 bamboo or wooden skewers in water for about 20 minutes. Drain and thread 4 shrimp onto each skewer.

4 Broil the skewers under a preheated hot broiler for 5–6 minutes, turning them over once, until they turn pink and begin to brown. Alternatively, barbecue over hot coals.

5 Thread a wedge of lime on to the end of each skewer and serve with crusty bread and salad.

Rice & Noodles

With it's monsoon climate and abundant rainfall, Thailand has the ideal conditions for rice growing, and has become one of the major rice producers in the world. It's even thought that rice grew there as far back as 3500 B.C. So, not surprisingly, rice is the main staple food in Thailand and hardly a meal goes by without it in some form or another.

Two main varieties of rice are used in Thai cooking—a long and a short grain. The long grain is Thai fragrant rice, a good-quality white, fluffy rice with delicately scented, separate grains. Glutinous or "sticky" rice is a round grain rice with a high starch content which causes the grains to stick together.

Noodles also play a vital part in Thai meals, and street vendors serve them as a snack at all times of day. Rice noodles in flat ribbons or thin vermicelli are the most common, and need to be soaked before being fried or added to soups and stir fries. Cellophane (mung beans) noodles are also locally made, but egg noodles are often imported from China. Most noodle dishes are served with an array of condiments for the diner to add to his or her taste—usually including crushed dried chilies, finely chopped peanuts, Thai fish sauce, soy sauce, and sugar.

Crispy Rice Noodles

This is a version of a favorite Thai dish, "mee krob," one of those exciting dishes which varies from one household to another and one day to the next—depending on the ingredients available.

Serves 4

INGREDIENTS

vegetable oil for deep frying, plus
   1½ tbsp.
7 oz. rice vermicelli noodles
1 onion, finely chopped
4 garlic cloves, finely chopped
1 boneless, skinless chicken breast,
   finely chopped
2 red bird's eye chilies, deseeded
   and sliced

4 tbsp. dried black mushrooms, soaked
   and thinly sliced
3 tbsp. dried shrimp
4 scallions, sliced
3 tbsp. lime juice
2 tbsp. soy sauce
2 tbsp. Thai fish sauce
2 tbsp. rice vinegar

2 tbsp. soft light brown sugar
2 eggs, beaten
3 tbsp. chopped fresh cilantro

TO GARNISH:
scallion curls
cilantro sprigs

1 Heat the oil in a wok until very hot and deep-fry the noodles quickly, turning them occasionally, until puffed up, crisp and pale golden brown. Lift on to paper towels and drain thoroughly.

2 Heat 1 tablespoon oil and fry the onion and garlic for 1 minute. Add the chicken and stir-fry for about 3 minutes. Stir in the chilies, mushrooms, shrimp, and scallions.

3 Mix together the lime juice, soy sauce, fish sauce, rice vinegar, and sugar, then stir into the pan and cook for an additional minute. Remove the wok from the heat.

4 Heat the remaining oil in a wide pan and pour in the eggs to coat the base of the pan evenly, making a thin omelette. Cook until set and golden, then turn it over and cook the other side. Turn out and roll up, then slice into long ribbon strips.

5 Toss together the fried noodles, stir-fried ingredients, cilantro, and omelette strips. Garnish with scallion curls and cilantro leaves.

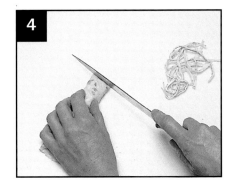

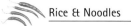

Sesame Noodles with Shrimp and Cilantro

Delicately scented with sesame and cilantro,
these noodles make an unusual lunch or supper dish.

Serves 4

INGREDIENTS

1 garlic clove, chopped
1 scallion, chopped
1 small red chili, deseeded and sliced
1 handful fresh cilantro
10½ oz. fine egg noodles

2 tbsp. vegetable oil
1 tsp. shrimp paste
2 tsp. sesame oil
1½ cups peeled, raw shrimp
2 tbsp. lime juice

2 tbsp. Thai fish sauce
1 tsp. sesame seeds, toasted

1 Place the garlic, onion, chili, and cilantro into a mortar and pestle and grind to a smooth paste.

2 Drop the noodles into a pan of boiling water and bring back to a boil, then simmer for 4 minutes, or according to the package directions.

3 Meanwhile, heat the oil in a wok and stir in the shrimp paste and ground cilantro mixture.

Stir over a medium heat for 1 minute.

4 Stir in the shrimp and stir-fry for 2 minutes. Stir in the lime juice and fish sauce and cook for an additional minute.

5 Drain the noodles and toss them into the wok. Sprinkle with the sesame seeds and serve.

COOK'S TIP

The roots of cilantro are widely used in Thai cooking, so if you can buy fresh cilantro with the root attached the whole plant can be used in this dish for maximum flavor. If not, just use the stems and leaves.

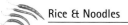

Hot & Sour Noodles

This simple, fast-food dish is sold from street food stalls in Thailand, with many and varied additions of meat and vegetables. It is equally good served hot or cold.

Serves 4

INGREDIENTS

9 oz. dried medium egg noodles
1 tbsp. sesame oil
1 tbsp. chili oil
1 garlic clove, crushed
2 scallions, finely chopped
²/₃ cup button mushrooms, sliced

1 cup dried Chinese black mushrooms,
  soaked, drained, and sliced
2 tbsp. lime juice
3 tbsp. light soy sauce
1 tsp. sugar

TO SERVE:
shredded Chinese cabbage
2 tbsp. chopped cilantro
2 tbsp. toasted peanuts

1 Cook the noodles in a large pan of boiling water for 3–4 minutes, or according to the package directions. Drain well, then toss with the sesame oil and set aside.

2 Heat the chili oil in a large wok and quickly stir-fry the garlic, onions, and button mushrooms to soften.

3 Add the black mushrooms, lime juice, soy sauce, and

sugar and continue stir-frying until boiling. Add the noodles and toss to mix. Serve spooned over Chinese cabbage, sprinkled with cilantro and peanuts.

COOK'S TIP

Thai chili oil is very hot, so if you want a milder flavor use vegetable oil for the initial cooking instead, then add a final dribble of chili oil just for seasoning.

Pad Thai Noodles

The combination of ingredients in this classic noodle dish varies depending on the cook, but it commonly contains a mixture of pork and shrimp or other seafood.

Serves 4

INGREDIENTS

9 oz. rice stick noodles
3 tbsp. peanut oil
3 garlic cloves, finely chopped
4½ oz. pork tenderloin, chopped into
   ¼ inch pieces
1¼ cups peeled shrimp

1 tbsp. sugar
3 tbsp. Thai fish sauce
1 tbsp. tomato ketchup
1 tbsp. lime juice
2 eggs, beaten
generous 1 cup bean sprouts

TO GARNISH:
1 tsp. dried red chili flakes
2 scallions, thickly sliced
2 tbsp. chopped fresh cilantro

1 Soak the rice noodles in hot water for about 15 minutes, or according to the package directions.

2 Heat the oil in a wok and fry the garlic over a high heat for 30 seconds. Stir in the pork and stir-fry for 2-3 minutes until lightly browned.

3 Stir in the shrimp, then add the sugar, fish sauce, ketchup, and lime juice and continue stir-frying for 30 seconds.

4 Stir in the eggs and stir-fry until lightly set. Stir in the noodles, then add the bean sprouts and stir-fry for 30 seconds to cook lightly.

5 Turn out on to a serving dish and scatter with chili flakes, scallions and cilantro.

COOK'S TIP

Drain the rice noodles before adding to the pan, as excess moisture will spoil the texture of the dish.

Rice Noodles with Mushrooms & Tofu

An alternative to classic dishes such as Pad Thai Noodles (page 134), this quick and easy dish is very filling. If you omit the fish sauce, it can be served as a vegetarian dish.

Serves 4

INGREDIENTS

8 oz. rice stick noodles
2 tbsp. vegetable oil
1 garlic clove, finely chopped
¾ inch piece fresh ginger, finely
   chopped
4 shallots, thinly sliced

¾ cup shiitake mushrooms, sliced
½ cup firm tofu, cut into ⁵/₈ in. dice
2 tbsp. light soy sauce
1 tbsp. rice wine
1 tbsp. Thai fish sauce
1 tbsp. smooth peanut butter

1 tsp. chili sauce
2 tbsp. chopped toasted peanuts
basil leaves, to serve

1 Soak the rice noodles in hot water for 15 minutes, or according to the package directions. Drain well.

2 Heat the oil in a wok and stir-fry the garlic, ginger, and shallots for 1–2 minutes until softened and lightly browned.

3 Add the mushrooms and stir-fry for an additional 2–3 minutes. Stir in the tofu and toss gently to brown lightly.

4 Mix together the soy sauce, rice wine, fish sauce, peanut butter, and fish sauce, then stir into the pan.

5 Stir in the rice noodles and toss to coat evenly in the sauce. Scatter with peanuts and basil and serve hot.

COOK'S TIP

For an easy pantry dish, replace the shiitake mushrooms with a can of Chinese straw mushrooms. Or, use dried shiitake mushrooms, soaked and drained before use.

Thai-style Noodles Rostis

Serves these crisp, fried "rosti" noodle pancakes as an unusual first course, or as a decorative side dish alongside meat dishes.

Serves 4

INGREDIENTS

4½ oz. vermicelli rice noodles
2 scallions, finely shredded
1 lemon grass stalk, finely shredded
3 tbsp. finely shredded fresh coconut
salt and pepper
vegetable oil for frying

TO SERVE:
generous 1 cup bean sprouts
1 small red onion, thinly sliced
1 avocado, thinly sliced

2 tbsp. lime juice
2 tbsp. rice wine
1 tsp. chili sauce

1 Break the rice noodles into short pieces and soak in hot water for 4 minutes, or according to the package directions. Drain thoroughly and pat dry with paper towels.

2 Stir together the noodles, scallions, lemon grass, and coconut.

3 Heat a small amount of oil until very hot in a heavy-based frying pan. Brush a 3½ inch round biscuit cutter with oil and place in the pan. Spoon a small amount of noodle mixture into the cutter to just cover the base of the pan, then press down lightly with the back of a spoon.

4 Fry for 30 seconds, then carefully remove the cutter and continue frying the rosti until it is golden brown, turning it over once. Remove and drain on paper towels. Repeat with the remaining noodles, to make about 12 rostis.

5 To serve, arrange the noodles in stacks, with bean sprouts, onion, and avocado between the layers. Mix the lime juice, rice wine, and chili sauce together and spoon over just before serving.

Drunken Noodles

Perhaps this would be more correctly named "drunkards' noodles," as it's a dish that is supposedly often eaten as a hangover cure—the fiery kick of the chilies wakes up the system and the lime leaf and basil cleanse and refresh the palate.

Serves 4

INGREDIENTS

6 oz. rice stick noodles
2 tbsp. vegetable oil
1 garlic clove, crushed
2 small green chilies, chopped
1 small onion, thinly sliced

5½ oz. lean ground pork or chicken
1 small green bell pepper, deseeded
  and finely chopped
4 kaffir lime leaves, finely shredded
1 tbsp. dark soy sauce

1 tbsp. light soy sauce
½ tsp. sugar
1 tomato, cut into thin wedges
2 tbsp. sweet basil leaves

1 Soak the rice sticks in hot water for 15 minutes, or according to the package directions. Drain well.

2 Heat the oil in a wok and stir-fry the garlic, chilies, and onion for 1 minute.

3 Stir in the pork or chicken and stir-fry on a high heat for an additional minute, then add the pepper and continue stir-frying for an additional 2 minutes or so.

4 Stir in the lime leaves, soy sauces, and sugar. Add the noodles and tomato and toss well to heat thoroughly.

5 Sprinkle with basil and serve immediately.

COOK'S TIP

Fresh kaffir lime leaves freeze well, if you buy more than you need—simply tie them in a tightly sealed plastic freezer bag and freeze for up to a month. They can be used straight from the freezer.

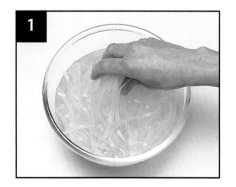

Crispy Duck with Noodles and Tamarind

A robustly flavored dish that makes a substantial main course.
Serve it with a refreshing cucumber salad or a light vegetable stir-fry.

Serves 4

INGREDIENTS

3 duck breasts, total weight about
   14 oz.
2 garlic cloves, crushed
1½ tsp. chili paste
1 tbsp. honey

3 tbsp. dark soy sauce
½ tsp. five-spice powder
9 oz. rice stick noodles
1 tsp. vegetable oil
1 tsp. sesame oil

2 scallions, sliced
3½ oz. snow peas
2 tbsp. tamarind juice

1 Prick the duck breast skin all over with a fork and place in a deep dish.

2 Mix together the garlic, chili, honey, soy sauce, and five-spice powder, then pour over the duck. Turn the breasts over to coat them evenly, then cover and leave to marinate in the refrigerator for at least 1 hour.

3 Meanwhile, soak the rice noodles in hot water for 15 minutes. Drain well.

4 Drain the duck breasts from the marinade and broil on a rack under high heat for about 10 minutes, turning them over occasionally, until they become a rich golden brown. Remove and slice the duck breasts thinly.

5 Heat the vegetable and sesame oils in a wok and toss the scallions and snow peas for 2 minutes. Stir in the reserved marinade and tamarind and bring to a boil.

6 Add the sliced duck and noodles and toss to heat thoroughly. Serve immediately.

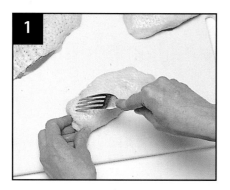

Rice Noodles with Chicken & Chinese Cabbage

The great thing about stir-fries is you can cook with very little fat and still get lots of flavor, as in this light, healthy lunch dish that's low in fat and very quick to make.

Serves 4

INGREDIENTS

7 oz. rice stick noodles
1 tbsp. sunflower oil
1 garlic clove, finely chopped
¾ inch piece fresh ginger, finely chopped
4 scallions, chopped
1 bird's eye red chili, deseeded and sliced

10½ oz. boneless, skinless chicken, finely chopped
2 chicken livers, finely chopped
1 celery stick, thinly sliced
1 carrot, cut into fine matchsticks
5½ cups shredded Chinese cabbage
4 tbsp. lime juice
2 tbsp. Thai fish sauce

1 tbsp. soy sauce

TO GARNISH:
2 tbsp. fresh chopped mint
slices of pickled garlic

1 Soak the rice noodles in hot water for 15 minutes, or according to the package directions. Drain well.

2 Heat the oil in a wok and stir-fry the garlic, ginger, scallions, and chili for about 1 minute. Stir in the chicken and chicken livers, then stir-fry over a high heat for 2–3 minutes until just beginning to brown.

3 Stir in the celery and carrot and stir-fry for 2 more minutes to soften. Add the Chinese cabbage, then stir in the lime juice, fish sauce, and soy sauce.

4 Add the noodles and stir to heat thoroughly. Sprinkle with mint and pickled garlic. Serve immediately.

Rice Noodles with Spinach

This quick stir-fried noodle dish is simple to prepare, and makes a delicious light lunch in minutes. You can leave out the dried shrimp, or replace them with chopped peanuts, for a vegetarian dish.

Serves 4

INGREDIENTS

4 oz. thin rice stick noodles
2 tbsp. dried shrimp (optional)
4 cups fresh young spinach
1 tbsp. peanut oil

2 garlic cloves, finely chopped
2 tsp. Thai green curry paste
1 tsp. sugar

1 tbsp. light soy sauce

1 Soak the noodles in hot water for 15 minutes, or according to the package directions, then drain well.

2 Soak the shrimp in hot water for 10 minutes and drain well. Wash the spinach thoroughly, drain well, and remove any tough stalks.

3 Heat the oil and stir-fry the garlic for 1 minute. Stir in the curry paste and stir-fry for 30 seconds. Stir in the soaked shrimp and stir-fry for 30 seconds.

4 Add the spinach and stir-fry for 1–2 minutes until the leaves are just wilted.

5 Stir in the sugar and soy sauce, then add the noodles and toss thoroughly to mix evenly. Serve hot.

COOK'S TIP

It is best to choose young spinach leaves for this dish, as they are beautifully tender and cook within a matter of seconds. If you can only get older spinach, however, shred the leaves before adding to the dish so they cook more quickly.

Egg Noodle Salad with Coconut, Lime, & Basil Dressing

A good dish for summer eating, this is light and refreshing in flavor and easy to cook. The turkey can be replaced with cooked chicken if you prefer.

Serves 4

INGREDIENTS

8 oz. dried egg noodles
2 tsp. sesame oil
1 carrot
1 cup bean sprouts
½ cucumber
5½ oz. cooked turkey breast meat, shredded into thin slivers

2 scallions, finely shredded
chopped peanuts and basil leaves, to garnish

DRESSING:
5 tbsp. coconut milk
3 tbsp. lime juice

1 tbsp. light soy sauce
2 tsp. Thai fish sauce
1 tsp. chili oil
1 tsp. sugar
2 tbsp. chopped cilantro
2 tbsp. chopped sweet basil

1 Cook the noodles in boiling water for 4 minutes, or according to the package directions. Plunge them into a bowl of cold water to cool, then rain and toss in sesame oil.

2 Use a vegetable peeler to shave off thin ribbons from the carrot. Blanch the ribbons and bean sprouts in boiling water for

30 seconds, then plunge into cold water for 30 seconds. Drain well. Shave thin ribbons of cucumber.

3 Toss the carrots, bean sprouts, and cucumber together with the turkey, scallions, and noodles.

4 Place all the dressing ingredients in a screw-top jar and shake well to mix evenly.

5 Toss the dressing into the noodle mixture, then pile on to a serving dish. Sprinkle with chopped peanuts and basil. Serve cold.

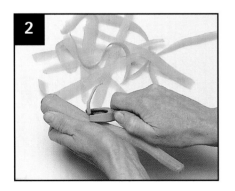

Stir-fried Rice with Egg Strips

Many Thai rice dishes are made from leftover rice that has been cooked for an earlier meal.
But nothing goes to waste, and it's often stir-fried with a few simple ingredients and aromatic
flavorings, as in this recipe. If you have any leftover vegetables or meat,
this is a good way to use them up.

Serves 4

INGREDIENTS

2 tbsp. peanut oil
1 egg, beaten with 1 tsp. water
1 garlic clove, finely chopped
1 small onion, finely chopped
1 tbsp. Thai red curry paste

2 cups cooked long-grain rice
$1/3$ cup cooked peas
1 tbsp. Thai fish sauce
2 tbsp. tomato ketchup
2 tbsp. chopped fresh cilantro

TO GARNISH:
cucumber slices
red chilies, cut into flowers

1 To make chili flowers, hold the stem with your fingertips and use a small sharp, pointed knife to cut a slit down the length from near the stem end to the tip. Turn the chili about a quarter turn and make another cut. Repeat to make a total of 4 cuts, then scrape out the seeds. Cut each "petal" again in half, or into quarters, to make 8–16 petals. Place in iced water.

2 Heat about 1 teaspoon of the oil in a wok. Pour in the egg mixture, swirling it to coat the pan evenly and make a thin layer. When set and golden, remove the egg from the pan and roll up. Keep to one side.

3 Add the remaining oil to the pan and stir-fry the garlic and onion for 1 minute. Add the curry paste, then stir in the rice and peas.

4 Stir in the fish sauce and ketchup. Remove the pan from the heat and pile rice on to a serving dish.

5 Slice the egg roll into spiral strips, without unrolling, and use to garnish the rice. Add cucumber slices and chili flowers.

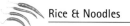
Jasmine Rice with Lemon and Basil

Jasmine rice has a delicate flavor and it can be served completely plain, with no other flavorings. This simple dish just has the light tang of lemon and soft scent of basil to add an extra touch.

Serves 4

INGREDIENTS

2 cups jasmine rice
3½ cups water

finely grated rind of ½ lemon

2 tbsp. chopped fresh sweet basil

1 Wash the rice in several changes of cold water until the water runs clear. Bring the water to a boil in a large pan, then add the rice.

2 Bring back to a rolling boil. Turn the heat to a low simmer, cover and simmer for an additional 12 minutes.

3 Remove the pan from the heat and leave to stand, covered, for 10 minutes.

4 Fluff up the rice with a fork, then stir in the lemon. Serve scattered with basil.

COOK'S TIP

It is important to leave the pan tightly covered while the rice cooks and steams inside so the grains cook evenly and become fluffy and separate.

Rice with Seafood

This soup-like main course rice dish is packed with fresh seafood, typically Thai in flavor.
If you have time, make your own fish stock from fish trimmings, or use good quality stock cubes.

Serves 4

INGREDIENTS

12 mussels in shell, cleaned
9 cups fish stock
2 tbsp. vegetable oil
1 garlic clove, crushed
1 tsp. grated fresh ginger
1 red bird's eye chili, chopped

2 scallions chopped
scant 1¼ cups long-grain rice
2 small squid, cleaned and sliced
3½ oz. firm white fish fillet, such as
    halibut or monkfish, cut into
    chunks

3½ oz. peeled raw shrimp
2 tbsp. Thai fish sauce
3 tbsp. chopped fresh cilantro

1 Discard any mussels with damaged shells or open ones that do not close with firmly tapped. Heat 4 tablespoons of the stock in a large pan. Add the mussels, cover and shake the pan until the mussels open. Remove from the heat and discard any which do not open.

2 Heat the oil in a large wok and fry the garlic, ginger, chili, and scallions for 30 seconds. Add the stock and bring to a boil.

3 Stir in the rice, then add the squid, fish fillet, and shrimp. Lower the heat and simmer gently for 15 minutes, or until the rice is cooked. Add the fish sauce and mussels.

4 Ladle into wide bowls and sprinkle with cilantro.

COOK'S TIP

You could use leftover, already-cooked rice for this dish. Just simmer the seafood gently until cooked, then stir in the rice at the end.

Coconut Rice with Pineapple

Cooking rice in coconut milk makes it very satisfying and nutritious, and often this is used as a base for main dishes, with the addition of meat, fish, vegetables or eggs to make it more substantial.

Serves 4

INGREDIENTS

1 cup long-grain rice
2¼ cups coconut milk
2 lemon grass stalks

scant 1 cup water
2 slices fresh pineapple, peeled and
diced

2 tbsp. shredded coconut, toasted
chili sauce, to serve

1 Wash the rice in several changes of cold water until the water runs clear. Place in a large pan with the coconut milk.

2 Place the lemon grass on a firm work surface and bruise it by hitting firmly with a meat hammer or rolling pin. Add to the pan with the rice and coconut milk.

3 Add the water and bring to a boil. Lower the heat, cover the pan tightly and simmer gently for 15 minutes. Remove the pan form the heat and fluff up the rice with a fork.

4 Remove the lemon grass and stir in the pineapple. Scatter with fresh coconut and serve with chili sauce.

VARIATION

A sweet version of this dish can be made by simply omitting the lemon grass and stirring in palm sugar or caster sugar to taste during cooking. Serve as a dessert, with extra pineapple slices.

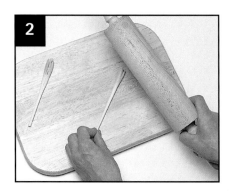

Vegetables & Salads

Many of the local vegetables, salad leaves, and shoots which Thais use in vegetable dishes and salads are native, often growing wild locally and uncultivated. This makes it difficult to produce really authentic Thai salads at home, as even the best Asian food stores can not source all the of these fresh ingredients.

We may be reduced to substituting a few fresh ingredients with canned ones, or local Thai vegetables with more familiar Western ones, but luckily we can now buy a good selection of cultivated Asian vegetables such as bok choi and Chinese cabbage. So, with a few careful choices, it's easy to produce some imaginative vegetable dishes with distinctly Thai flavors.

A Thai salad can make a stunning centerpiece for any dinner table. Thai cooks usually add strips or finely chopped cooked meat, fish or shellfish to their salads, or for vegetarian dishes, mushrooms or tofu will appear.

Dressings are typically piquant and spicy, with the usual skillful balance of bitter, salt, sour, hot, and sweet. To finish, a sprinkling of crushed peanuts or dried chilies, chopped cilantro or mint, or slices of pickled garlic, and a final flourish of chili flowers, scallion tassels, or other skillfully carved vegetables.

Crisp Pickled Vegetables

These crisp, delicately preserved vegetables are usually served as an accompaniment to fried meat or fish dishes. Thai cooks love to cut vegetables decoratively, and would typically cut the carrots into small flower shapes, but if you're short of time, thin slices look just fine.

Serves 6–8

INGREDIENTS

½ small cauliflower
½ cucumber
2 medium carrots
7 oz. green beans

½ small Chinese cabbage
2¼ cups rice vinegar
1 tbsp. sugar
1 tsp. salt

3 garlic cloves
3 shallots
3 bird's eye red chilies
5 tbsp. peanut oil

1 Trim the cauliflower. Peel and deseed the cucumber. Peel the carrots. Top and tail the beans. Trim the cabbage. Cut all the vegetables into bite-sized pieces. If you have time, cut the carrots into flower shapes.

2 Place the rice vinegar, sugar, and salt in a large pan and bring almost to a boil. Add the vegetables, lower the heat and simmer for 3–4 minutes until they are just tender, but still crisp inside. Remove the pan from the heat and leave the vegetables and vinegar to cool.

3 Peel the garlic and shallots and deseed the chilies. Place in a mortar and pestle and grind until a smooth paste forms.

4 Heat the oil in a wok and stir-fry the spice paste gently for 1–2 minutes. Add the vegetables with the vinegar and cook for an additional 2 minutes to reduce the liquid slightly. Remove from the heat and leave to cool.

5 Serve the pickles cold, or pack into jars and store in the refrigerator for up to 2 weeks.

COOK'S TIP

To make simple carrot flowers, peel the carrot thinly as usual, then use a small sharp knife to cut narrow "channels" down the length of it at regular intervals. Slice the carrot as usual and the slices will resemble flowers.

Chili & Coconut Sambal

A sweet-sour sambal that goes well with broiled or barbecued fish.
It can also be stirred into rice or noodles or curry dishes as extra flavoring.
Adjust the amount of chili to your own taste.

Serves 6-8

INGREDIENTS

1 small coconut
1 slice fresh pineapple, finely diced
1 small onion, finely chopped
2 small green chilies, deseeded and
    chopped

2 inch piece lemon grass
12 tsp. salt
1 tsp. shrimp paste
1 tbsp. lime juice

2 tbsp. chopped fresh cilantro
cilantro sprigs, to garnish

1 Puncture 2 of the coconut eyes with a screwdriver and pour the milk out from the shell. Crack the shell, prise away the flesh and coarsely grate it into a bowl.

2 Mix the coconut with the pineapple, onion, chilies, and lemon grass.

3 Blend together the salt, shrimp paste, and lime juice, then stir into the sambal.

4 Stir in the cilantro. Spoon into a small dish to serve.

COOK'S TIP

The coconut can be grated quickly by using a grating blade on a food processor.

VARIATION

To make a quicker version of this sambal, stir in a teaspoon of Thai green curry paste into freshly grated coconut and add finely diced pineapple and lime juice to taste.

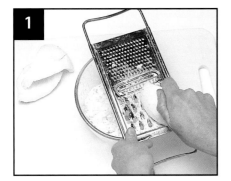

Mixed Vegetables in Peanut Sauce

This colorful mix of vegetables in a rich, spicy peanut sauce can be served either as a side dish or as a vegetarian main course.

Serves 4

INGREDIENTS

2 carrots, peeled
1 small head cauliflower, trimmed
2 small heads green bok choi
5½ oz. green beans, topped and tailed

2 tbsp. vegetable oil
1 garlic clove, finely chopped
6 scallions, sliced
1 tsp. chili paste

2 tbsp. soy sauce
2 tbsp. rice wine
4 tbsp. smooth peanut butter
3 tbsp. coconut milk

1 Cut the carrots diagonally into thin slices. Cut the cauliflower into small florets, then slice the stalk thinly. Thickly slice the bok choi. Cut the beans into 1¼ inch lengths.

2 Heat the oil in a wok and stir-fry the garlic and scallions for about 1 minute. Stir in the chili paste and cook for a few seconds.

3 Add the carrots and cauliflower and stir-fry for 2–3 minutes.

4 Add the bok choi and beans and stir-fry for an additional 2 minutes. Stir in the soy sauce and rice wine.

5 Mix the peanut butter with the coconut milk and stir into the pan, then cook, stirring, for an additional minute. Serve immediately.

COOK'S TIP

It's important to cut the vegetables thinly into even-sized pieces so they cook quickly and evenly. Prepare all the vegetables before you start to cook.

Thai Red Bean Curry

The "red" in the title refers not to the beans, but to the sauce, which has a warm, rusty red color.
This is a good way to serve not only fresh beans, but to lift the flavor of frozen beans, too.

Serves 4

INGREDIENTS

14 oz. green beans, topped and tailed
1 garlic clove, finely sliced
1 red bird's eye chili, deseeded and
  chopped
½ tsp. paprika pepper

1 piece lemon grass stalk, finely
  chopped
2 tsp. Thai fish sauce
½ cup coconut milk

1 tbsp. sunflower oil
2 scallions, sliced

1 Cut the beans into 2 inch pieces and cook in boiling water for 2 minutes. Drain well.

2 Place the garlic, chili, paprika, lemon grass, fish sauce, and coconut milk in a blender and process until a smooth paste forms.

3 Heat the oil and stir-fry the scallions over a high heat for about 1 minute. Add the paste and bring to a boil.

4 Simmer for 3–4 minutes to reduce by about half. Add the beans and simmer for an additional 1–2 minutes until tender. Serve hot.

COOK'S TIP

Young runner beans can be used instead of green beans. Remove any strings from the beans then cut at a diagonal angle in short lengths. Cook as above until tender.

Stir-Fried Ginger Mushrooms

*This quick vegetarian stir-fry is actually more like a rich curry,
with lots of warm spice and garlic, balanced with creamy coconut milk.*

Serves 4

INGREDIENTS

2 tbsp. vegetable oil
3 garlic cloves, crushed
1 tbsp. red Thai curry paste
½ tsp. turmeric
14/½ oz. can Chinese straw
   mushrooms, drained and halved

scant ½ cup coconut milk
¾ inch piece fresh ginger, finely
   shredded
1 cup Chinese dried black mushrooms,
   soaked, drained and sliced
1 tbsp. lemon juice

1 tbsp. light soy sauce
2 tsp. sugar
½ tsp. salt
8 cherry tomatoes, halved
cilantro leaves, to garnish
boiled fragrant rice, to serve

1 Heat the oil and fry the garlic for about 1 minute, stirring. Stir in the curry paste and turmeric and cook for about an additional 30 seconds.

2 Stir in the shiitake mushrooms and ginger and stir-fry for about 2 minutes. Stir in the coconut milk and bring to a boil.

3 Stir in the Chinese straw mushrooms, lemon juice, soy sauce, sugar, and salt and heat thoroughly. Add the tomatoes and toss gently to heat through.

4 Scatter the cilantro over and serve hot, with fragrant rice.

COOK'S TIP

You can vary the mushrooms depending on your own taste—try a mixture of oyster and shiitake for a change, or even just ordinary cultivated button mushrooms are very tasty cooked this way.

Thai-spiced Mushrooms

An unusual dish that makes a good vegetarian main course.
Serve the mushrooms with a colorful fresh salad.

Serves 4

INGREDIENTS

8 large, flat mushrooms
3 tbsp. sunflower oil
2 tbsp. light soy sauce
1 garlic clove, crushed

¾ inch piece fresh galangal or ginger, grated
1 tbsp. Thai green curry paste
8 baby corn, sliced

3 scallions, chopped
generous 1 cup bean sprouts
3½ oz. firm tofu, diced
2 tsp. sesame seeds, toasted

1 Remove the stalks from the mushrooms and set aside. Place the caps on a baking sheet. Mix 2 tablespoons of the oil with 1 tablespoon of the light soy sauce and brush over the mushrooms.

2 Broil under high heat until golden and tender, turning them over once.

3 Meanwhile, chop the mushroom stalks finely. Heat the remaining oil and stir-fry the stalks with the garlic and galangal or ginger for 1 minute. Stir in the curry paste, baby corn, and scallions and stir-fry for 1 minute.

4 Add the bean sprouts and stir for an additional minute.

5 Add the tofu and remaining soy sauce, then toss lightly to heat. Spoon the mixture into the mushroom caps. Sprinkle with the sesame seeds. Serve immediately.

COOK'S TIP

Galangal or ginger can be frozen for several weeks, either peeled and finely chopped ready to add to dishes, or in a whole piece. Thaw the piece or grate finely from frozen.

Asian Vegetables with Yellow Bean Sauce

Serve this colorful mixture with a pile of golden, crispy noodles as a main course, or on it's own to accompany meat dishes.

Serves 4

INGREDIENTS

1 eggplant
salt
2 tbsp. vegetable oil
3 garlic cloves, crushed
4 scallions, chopped
1 small red bell pepper, deseeded and
    thinly sliced
4 baby corn, halved lengthways

2 cups coarsely shredded Chinese
    mustard greens
1 cup snow peas
14½ oz. can Chinese straw
    mushrooms, drained
generous 1 cup bean sprouts
2 tbsp. rice wine
2 tbsp. yellow bean sauce

2 tbsp. dark soy sauce
1 tsp. chili sauce
1 tsp. sugar
½ cup chicken or vegetable stock
1 tsp. cornstarch
2 tsp. water

1 Trim the eggplant and cut into 2 inch long matchsticks. Place in a colander, sprinkle with salt and leave to drain for 30 minutes. Rinse in cold water and pat dry with paper towels.

2 Heat the oil in a wok and stir-fry the garlic, scallions, and bell pepper over a high heat for 1 minute. Stir in the eggplant pieces and stir-fry for an additional minute, or until softened.

3 Stir in the corn and snow peas and stir-fry for about 1 minute. Add the mustard greens, mushrooms, and bean sprouts and stir-fry for 30 seconds.

4 Mix together the rice wine, yellow bean sauce, soy sauce, chili sauce, and sugar and add to the pan with the stock. Bring to a boil, stirring.

5 Blend the cornstarch with the water to form a smooth paste. Stir quickly into the wok and cook for an additional minute. Serve immediately.

Potatoes in Creamed Coconut

A colorful way to serve potatoes that is quick and easy to make.
Serve it with spicy meat curries with a salad on the side.

Serves 4

INGREDIENTS

1 lb. 5 oz. potatoes
1 onion, thinly sliced
2 bird's eye red chilies, chopped
½ tsp. salt

½ tsp. ground black pepper
½ cup creamed coconut
1½ cups vegetable or chicken stock

chopped fresh cilantro or basil, to
garnish

1 Peel the potatoes thinly and cut into ¾ inch chunks.

2 Place the potatoes in a pan with the onion, chili, salt, pepper, and creamed coconut. Stir in the stock.

3 Bring to a boil, stirring, then lower the heat, cover and simmer gently, stirring occasionally, until the potatoes are tender.

4 Adjust the seasoning to taste, then sprinkle with chopped cilantro or basil. Serve hot.

COOK'S TIP

If the potatoes are a thin-skinned, or a new variety, simply wash or scrub to remove any dirt and cook with the skins on. This adds extra dietary fiber and nutrients to the finished dish, and cuts down on the preparation time. Baby new potatoes can be cooked whole.

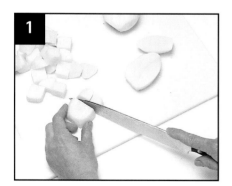

Stir-fried Broccoli in Oyster Sauce

Chinese oyster sauce has a sweet-salty flavor, ideal for adding a richly Asian flavor to plain vegetables. Try this recipe with fresh asparagus when it's in season.

Serves 4

INGREDIENTS

14 oz. broccoli

1 tbsp. peanut oil

2 shallots, finely chopped

1 garlic clove, finely chopped

1 tbsp. rice wine or sherry

5 tbsp. oyster sauce

¼ tsp. ground black pepper

1 tsp. chili oil

1 Trim the broccoli and cut into small florets. Blanch in boiling water for 30 seconds, then drain well.

2 Heat the oil in a wok and stir-fry the shallots and garlic for 1–2 minutes until golden brown.

3 Stir in the broccoli and stir-fry for 2 minutes. Add the rice wine and oyster sauce and stir for an additional 1 minute.

4 Stir in the pepper and drizzle with a little chili oil just before serving.

COOK'S TIP

To make chili oil, tuck fresh red or green chilies into a jar and top up with olive or a light vegetable oil. Cover with a lid and leave to infuse the flavor for at least 3 weeks before using.

Roasted Thai-spiced Peppers

A colorful side dish that also makes a good buffet party salad.
This is best made in advance to give time for the flavors to mingle.

Serves 4

INGREDIENTS

2 red bell peppers
2 yellow bell peppers
2 green bell peppers

2 red bird's eye chilies, deseeded and
  finely chopped
1 lemon grass stalk, finely shredded

4 tbsp. lime juice
2 tbsp. palm (or dark brown) sugar
1 tbsp. Thai fish sauce

1 Roast the peppers under a hot broiler, barbecue over hot coals or roast in a hot oven, turning them over occasionally, until the skins are charred. Cool slightly, then remove the skins. Cut each in half and remove the core and seeds.

2 Slice the peppers thickly and arrange in a wide serving dish.

3 Place the chilies, lemon grass, lime juice, sugar, and fish sauce in a screw-top jar and shake well until thoroughly mixed.

4 Pour the dressing evenly over the peppers. Allow to cool completely, cover with plastic wrap and chill in the refrigerator for at least an hour before serving.

COOK'S TIP

The flavors will mingle better if the peppers are still slightly warm when you spoon the dressing over, so prepare the dressing while the peppers are cooking, so it's ready to spoon over.

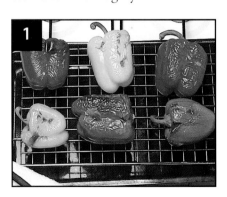

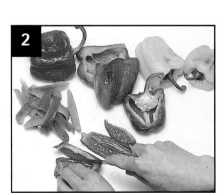

Bok Choi with Crab Meat

Bok choi, also called pak choy or Chinese chard, has a delicate, fresh flavor and crisp texture, which is best retained by light, quick cooking. This makes it an ideal choice for stir-frying.

Serves 4

INGREDIENTS

2 heads green bok choi, about 9 oz.
   total weight
2 tbsp. vegetable oil

1 garlic clove, thinly sliced
2 tbsp. oyster sauce
1 cup cherry tomatoes, halved

6 oz. can white crab meat, drained
salt and pepper

1 Trim the bok choi and cut into 1 inch thick slices.

2 Heat the oil in a wok and stir-fry the garlic quickly over a high heat for 1 minute.

3 Add the bok choi and stir-fry for 2–3 minutes until the leaves wilt, but the stalks are still crisp.

4 Add the oyster sauce and tomatoes and stir-fry for an additional minute.

5 Add the crab meat and season well with salt and pepper. Heat thoroughly before serving.

VARIATION

For a vegetarian version of this dish, omit the crab meat and replace the oyster sauce with 2 tablespoons of light soy sauce.

VARIATION

If pak choi is not available, cabbage makes a good alternative for this dish.

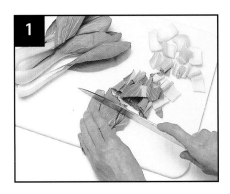

Spiced Cashew Nut Curry

This unusual vegetarian dish is best served a side dish
with other curries, either vegetable or meat-based, with rice to soak up
the wonderfully rich, spiced juices.

Serves 4

INGREDIENTS

1½ cups unsalted cashew nuts
1 tsp. coriander seeds
1 tsp. cumin seeds
2 cardamom pods, crushed
1 tbsp. sunflower oil
1 onion, finely sliced

1 garlic clove, crushed
1 small green chili, deseeded and
    chopped
1 cinnamon stick
½ tsp. ground turmeric
4 tbsp. coconut cream

1¼ cups hot vegetable stock
3 kaffir lime leaves, finely shredded
salt and pepper
boiled jasmine rice, to serve

1 Soak the cashew nuts overnight in cold water to just cover. Drain thoroughly. Crush the coriander cumin seeds, and cardamom pods in a mortar and pestle.

2 Heat the oil and stir-fry the onion and garlic for 2–3 minutes to soften, but not brown. Add the chili, crushed spices, cinnamon stick, and turmeric and stir-fry for an additional minute.

3 Add the coconut cream and the hot stock to the pan. Bring to a boil, then add the cashew nuts and lime leaves.

4 Cover the pan, lower the heat and simmer for about 20 minutes. Serve with jasmine rice.

COOK'S TIP

All spices give the best flavor when freshly crushed, but if you prefer, you can use ground spices instead.

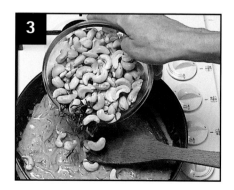

Potato & Spinach Yellow Curry

Potatoes are not highly regarded in Thai cookery, as rice is the traditional staple.
This dish is a tasty exception, and with it's luxuriously creamy, golden coconut sauce,
it makes a superb side dish for any meal.

Serves 4

INGREDIENTS

2 garlic cloves, finely chopped
1¼ inch piece galangal, finely
  chopped
1 lemon grass stem, finely chopped
1 tsp. coriander seeds
3 tbsp. vegetable oil

2 tsp. red curry paste
½ tsp. turmeric
scant 1 cup coconut milk
9 oz. potatoes, peeled and cut into ¾
  inch cubes
scant ½ cup vegetable stock

7 oz. (3 cups) young spinach leaves
1 small onion, thinly sliced into rings

1 Place the garlic, galangal, lemon grass, and coriander seeds in a mortar and pestle and pound until a smooth paste forms.

2 Heat 2 tablespoons of the oil in a wok. Stir in the paste and stir-fry for 30 seconds. Stir in the curry paste and turmeric, then add the coconut milk and bring to a boil.

3 Add the potatoes and stock. Return to a boil, then lower the heat and simmer, uncovered, for 10–12 minutes until the potatoes are almost tender.

4 Stir in the spinach and simmer until the leaves are wilted.

5 Meanwhile, fry the onions in the remaining oil until crisp

and golden brown. Place on top of the curry just before serving.

COOK'S TIP

Choose a firm, waxy potato for this dish, one that will keep it's shape during cooking, in preference to a floury variety which can break up easily.

Sweet Potato Cakes with Soy-Tomato Sauce

Enticing little tasty mouthfuls of sweet potato, served hot and sizzling from the pan with a delicious fresh tomato sauce.

Serves 4

INGREDIENTS

2 sweet potatoes, 1 lb. 2 oz. total weight
2 garlic cloves, crushed
1 small green chili, chopped
2 sprigs cilantro, chopped
1 tbsp. dark soy sauce
all-purpose flour for shaping

vegetable oil for frying
sesame seeds to sprinkle

SOY-TOMATO SAUCE:
2 tsp. vegetable oil
1 garlic clove, finely chopped

¾ inch piece fresh ginger, finely chopped
3 tomatoes, skinned and chopped
2 tbsp. dark soy sauce
1 tbsp. lime juice
2 tbsp. chopped fresh cilantro

1 First make the tomato sauce. Heat the oil in a wok and stir-fry the garlic and ginger for about 1 minute. Add the tomatoes and stir-fry for an additional 2 minutes. Remove from the heat and stir in the soy sauce, lime, and cilantro. Set aside and keep warm.

2 Peel the sweet potatoes and grate finely (you can do this more quickly with a food processor). Place the garlic, chili, and cilantro in a mortar and pestle and crush to a smooth paste. Stir in the soy sauce.

3 Divide the mixture into 12 equal portions and shape each with your hands into a flat, round patty shape. Dip into flour and pat into shape.

4 Heat a shallow layer of oil in a wide frying pan. Fry the sweet potato patties over a high heat until golden, turning once. Drain on paper towels and sprinkle with sesame seeds. Serve hot, with a spoonful of the tomato sauce.

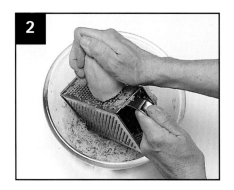

Thai-style Corn Fritters

These quick, little fritters can be served as a side dish or a first course, with a spoonful of spicy chili relish and a squeeze of lime juice.

Serves 4

INGREDIENTS

½ cup all-purpose flour
1 large egg
2 tsp. Thai green curry paste
5 tbsp. coconut milk
2¼ cups canned or frozen corn
   kernels

4 scallions
1 tbsp. chopped fresh cilantro
1 tbsp. chopped fresh basil
salt and pepper
vegetable oil for shallow frying

TO SERVE:
lime wedges
chili relish

1 Place the flour, egg, curry paste, coconut milk, and about half the corn kernels in a food processor and process until a smooth, thick batter forms.

2 Finely chop the scallions and stir into the batter with the remaining corn, chopped cilantro, and basil. Season well with salt and pepper.

3 Heat a small amount of oil in a wide, heavy-based frying pan. Drop tablespoonfuls of the batter into the pan and cook for 2–3 minutes until golden brown.

4 Turn them over and cook for an additional 2–3 minutes on the other side. Fry in batches, making about 12–16 fritters, keeping the cooked fritters hot while you cook the remaining batter. Serve the fritters hot, with lime wedges and a chili relish.

COOK'S TIP

If you prefer to use fresh corn instead of canned or frozen, strip the kernels from the cobs with a sharp knife, then cook in rapidly boiling water for about 2–3 minutes. Drain well before use.

Spicy Vegetable Fritters with Sweet Chili Dip

These spicy fritters show a clear Indian influence, as they are very similar to pakoras, which are spicy Indian vegetable fritters. They can be served as an first course or as a side dish. The sweet chili dip is a perfect partner.

Serves 4-6

INGREDIENTS

1 cup all-purpose flour
1 tsp. ground coriander
1 tsp. ground cumin
1 tsp. turmeric
1 tsp. salt
½ tsp. ground black pepper
2 garlic cloves, finely chopped
1¼ inch piece fresh ginger, chopped
2 small green chilies, finely chopped

1 tbsp. chopped fresh cilantro
about 1 cup water
1 onion, chopped
1 potato, coarsely grated
½ cup corn kernels
1 small eggplant, diced
1 cup Chinese broccoli, cut into short
   lengths
coconut oil for deep frying

SWEET CHILI DIP:
2 bird's eye red chilies, finely chopped
4 tbsp. sugar
4 tbsp. rice vinegar
1 tbsp. light soy sauce

1 Make the dip by mixing together all the ingredients thoroughly until the sugar is dissolved. Cover and set aside until needed.

2 For the fritters, place the flour in a bowl and stir in the coriander, cumin, turmeric, salt, and pepper. Add the garlic, ginger, chilies, and cilantro with just enough cold water to make a thick batter.

3 Add the onion, potato, corn, eggplant, and broccoli to the batter and stir well to distribute evenly.

4 Heat the oil in a wok to 375° F, or until a cube of bread browns in 40 seconds. Drop tablespoons of the batter into the hot oil and fry in batches until golden brown and crisp, turning once. Fry in batches, if necessary, and keep any fried fritters hot in a warm oven.

5 Drain well on paper towels. Serve with the dip.

Eggplant- & Mushroom-Stuffed Omelette

*In Thailand, egg dishes such as this one are eaten as main dishes or snacks,
depending on the time of day.*

Serves 1-2

INGREDIENTS

3 tbsp. vegetable oil
1 garlic clove, finely chopped
1 small onion, finely chopped
1 small eggplant, diced
½ small green bell pepper, deseeded
  and chopped

1 large dried black Chinese
  mushroom, soaked, drained and
  sliced
1 tomato, diced
1 tbsp. light soy sauce

½ tsp. sugar
¼ tsp. ground black pepper
2 large eggs
salad leaves, to garnish

1 Heat half the oil in a wok and fry the garlic over a high heat for 30 seconds. Add the onion and eggplant and continue to stir-fry until golden.

2 Add the green bell pepper and stir-fry for an additional minute to soften. Stir in the mushroom, tomato, soy sauce, sugar, and pepper. Remove from the pan and keep hot.

3 Beat the eggs together lightly. Heat the remaining oil, swirling to coat a wide area. Pour in the egg and swirl to set around the pan.

4 When the egg is set, spoon the filling into the center. Fold in the sides of the omelette to make a square bundle.

5 Slide the omelette carefully on to a warmed dish and garnish with salad leaves. Serve immediately.

COOK'S TIP

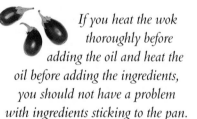

If you heat the wok thoroughly before adding the oil and heat the oil before adding the ingredients, you should not have a problem with ingredients sticking to the pan.

Crispy Tofu with Chili Soy Sauce

Tempting golden cubes of golden-fried tofu with colorful fresh carrot and peppers combine with a warm ginger sauce to make an unusual side dish or light lunch dish.

Serves 4

INGREDIENTS

10½ oz. firm tofu
2 tbsp. vegetable oil
1 garlic clove, sliced
1 carrot, cut into matchsticks

½ green bell pepper, deseeded and
  cut into matchsticks
1 red bird's eye chili, deseeded and
  finely chopped

2 tbsp. soy sauce
1 tbsp. lime juice
1 tbsp. Thai fish sauce
1 tbsp. soft light brown sugar
pickled ginger slices, to serve

1 Drain the tofu and pat dry with paper towels. Cut into ¾ inch cubes.

2 Heat the oil in a wok and stir-fry the garlic for 1 minute. Remove the garlic and add the tofu, then fry quickly until well-browned, turning gently to brown on all sides.

3 Lift out the tofu, drain and keep hot. Stir the carrot and peppers into the pan and stir-fry for 1 minute.

4 Pile the tofu on to a dish and spoon the carrot and peppers on the top.

5 Mix together the chili, soy sauce, lime juice, fish sauce, and sugar, stirring until the sugar is dissolved. Spoon over the tofu and serve topped with slices of pickled garlic.

COOK'S TIP

Make sure to buy firm fresh tofu for this dish—the softer "silken" type is not firm enough to hold it's shape well during frying . It is better for adding to soups.

Cucumber Salad

This recipe makes a good accompaniment for spicy broiled fish and meat dishes.
Once made, it can be chilled with the dressing for 1–2 hours, but is best eaten on the day of making.

Serves 4

INGREDIENTS

1 cucumber
salt and pepper
1 small red onion

1 garlic clove, crushed
½ tsp. chili paste
2 tsp. Thai fish sauce

1 tbsp. lime juice
1 tsp. sesame oil

1 Trim the cucumber and coarsely grate the flesh. Place in a colander over a bowl, sprinkle with 1 teaspoon salt and leave to drain for 20 minutes. Discard the liquid.

2 Peel the onion and chop finely, then toss into the cucumber. Spoon into 4 individual bowls or one large one.

3 Mix together the garlic, chili paste, fish sauce, lime juice, and sesame oil, then spoon over the salad. Cover and chill before serving.

VARIATION

For a change, peel the cucumber and cut it into small dice, then salt and drain as above. Drain and toss with the onions and dressing as before.

COOK'S TIP

Once the salad is made, it can be chilled with the dressing for 1–2 hours, but it is best eaten on the day of making

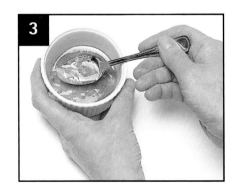

Thai Green Salad

An unusual side salad that is a good accompaniment to any simple Thai main dish, especially broiled meats and fish. Add the dressing just before serving or the leaves will lose their crispness.

Serves 4-6

INGREDIENTS

1 small head romaine lettuce
1 bunch scallions
½ cucumber
4 tbsp. coarsely shredded fresh
coconut, toasted

DRESSING:
4 tbsp. lime juice
2 tbsp. Thai fish sauce
1 small bird's eye chili, finely chopped
1 tsp. sugar

1 garlic clove, crushed
2 tbsp. chopped fresh cilantro
1 tbsp. chopped fresh mint

1 Tear or roughly shred the lettuce leaves and place in a large salad bowl.

2 Trim and thinly slice the scallions diagonally and add to the salad bowl.

3 Use a vegetable peeler to shave thin slices along the length of the cucumber and add to the salad bowl.

4 Place all the ingredients for the dressing in a screw-top jar and shake well to mix thoroughly.

5 Pour the dressing over the salad and toss well to coat the leaves evenly. Scatter the coconut over the salad and toss in lightly just before serving.

COOK'S TIP

This salad is good for picnics—to pack it easily, pack the leaves into a large plastic container or unbreakable salad bowl, then nestle the screw-top jar of dressing in the center. Cover with a lid or plastic wrap. Packed this way, the salad stays crisp and even if the dressing leaks during transit, there's no nasty mess.

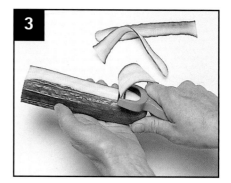

Grilled Eggplant & Sesame Salad

*Eggplants are a popular vegetable in Thailand,
as they grow easily throughout the Far East. This dish works well as a first course,
but can also be served as an accompaniment to fish or meat dishes.*

Serves 4

INGREDIENTS

8 baby eggplants
salt
2 tsp. chili oil
1 tbsp. soy sauce
1 tbsp. Thai fish sauce

1 garlic clove, thinly sliced
1 red bird's eye chili, deseeded and
  sliced
1 tbsp. sunflower oil
1 tsp. sesame oil

1 tbsp. lime juice
1 tsp. soft light brown sugar
1 tbsp. fresh chopped mint
1 tbsp. sesame seeds, toasted
mint leaves, to garnish

1 Cut the eggplants lengthways into thin slices to within 1 inch of the stem end. Place in a colander, sprinkling with salt between the slices and leave to drain for about 30 minutes. Rinse in cold water and pat dry with paper towels.

2 Mix the chili oil, soy sauce, and fish sauce together, then brush over the eggplants. Cook under a hot broiler, or barbecue over hot coals, for 6–8 minutes, turning them over occasionally and brushing with more chili oil glaze, until golden brown and softened. Arrange on a serving platter.

3 Fry the garlic and chili in the sunflower oil for 1–2 minutes until just beginning to brown. Remove the pan from the heat and add the sesame oil, lime juice, brown sugar, and any spare chili-oil glaze.

4 Add the chopped mint to the pan and spoon the warm dressing over the eggplants. Leave to marinate for about 20 minutes, then sprinkle with toasted sesame seeds. Serve garnished with mint.

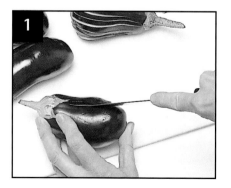

Asian Lettuce Cups

A crisp salad with a rich and warmly spiced coconut and peanut dressing, served in pretty lettuce cups.

Serves 4

INGREDIENTS

8 leaves romaine lettuce, or similar
   firm lettuce leaves
2 carrots
2 celery sticks
3½ oz. baby corn
2 scallions

1 cup bean sprouts
2 tbsp. chopped roasted peanuts

DRESSING:
2 tbsp. smooth peanut butter
3 tbsp. lime juice

3 tbsp. coconut milk
2 tsp. Thai fish sauce
1 tsp. sugar
1 tsp. grated fresh ginger
¼ tsp. Thai red curry paste

1 Wash and trim the lettuce leaves, leaving them whole. Arrange on a serving plate or on individual plates.

2 Trim the carrots and celery and cut into fine matchsticks. Trim the corn and onions and slice both diagonally.

3 Toss together all the vegetables with the bean sprouts. Divide between the lettuce cups.

4 To make the dressing, place all the ingredients in a screw-top jar and shake well until thoroughly mixed.

5 Spoon the dressing evenly over the salad cups and sprinkle with chopped peanuts. Serve immediately.

COOK'S TIP

Choose leaves with a deep cup shape to hold the salad neatly. If you prefer, Chinese cabbage may be used in place of the romaine lettuce. To remove the leaves from the whole head without tearing them, cut a thick slice from the base end so the leaves are not attached by their stems, then gently ease away the leafy parts.

Thai-style Carrot & Mango Salad

A wonderfully refreshing, simple salad to serve as a side dish with hot and spicy meat or fish dishes. It can be prepared an hour or two in advance of serving, and chilled in the refrigerator until needed.

Serves 4

INGREDIENTS

4 carrots
1 small, ripe mango
7 oz. firm tofu
1 tbsp. chopped fresh chives

DRESSING:
2 tbsp. orange juice
1 tbsp. lime juice
1 tsp. clear honey

½ tsp. orange-flower water
1 tsp. sesame oil
1 tsp. toasted sesame seeds

1 Peel and coarsely grate the carrots. Peel, pit, and thinly slice the mango.

2 Cut the tofu into ½ inch dice and toss together with the carrots and mango in a wide salad bowl.

3 For the dressing, place all the ingredients in a screw-top jar and shake well to mix evenly.

4 Pour the dressing over the salad and toss well to mix evenly.

5 Just before serving, toss the salad lightly and sprinkle with chives. Serve immediately.

COOK'S TIP

A food processor will grate the carrots in seconds, and is especially useful for time-saving if you're catering for a crowd.

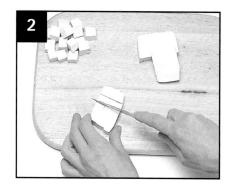

Bamboo Shoot Salad

In Thailand, fresh bamboo would always be used for this salad, but canned bamboo shoots make a very good alternative. This dish is usually served to accompany roast pork.

Serves 4

INGREDIENTS

2 shallots
2 garlic cloves
2 tbsp. Thai fish sauce
3 tbsp. lime juice
½ tsp. dried chili flakes

1 tsp. granulated sugar
1 tbsp. round grain rice
2 tsp. sesame seeds
12 oz. can bamboo shoots, drained
2 scallions, chopped

shredded Chinese cabbage or lettuce,
  to serve
mint leaves, to garnish

1 Place the whole shallots and garlic under a medium-hot broiler and broil until charred on the outside and tender inside. Remove the skins and place the flesh in a mortar and pestle. Crush to a smooth paste.

2 Mix the paste with the fish sauce, lime juice, chili flakes, and sugar.

3 Place the rice and sesame seeds in a heavy-based frying pan over the heat and cook to a rich golden brown, shaking the pan to brown evenly. Remove from the heat and crush lightly in a mortar and pestle.

4 Use a sharp knife to shred the bamboo shoots into fine matchsticks. Stir in the shallot and garlic dressing, tossing well to coat evenly. Stir in the toasted rice and sesame, then the scallions.

5 Pile the salad on to a serving dish and surround with shredded Chinese cabbage. Garnish with mint leaves and serve.

Hot & Sour Beef Salad

Thais are primarily fish-eaters, so beef usually only appears on the menu for feast days. But, as in this dish, a little can go a long way and Thais expertly extend it with exotic mixes of herbs, spices and colorful vegetables.

Serves 4

INGREDIENTS

1 tsp. black peppercorns
1 tsp. coriander seeds
1 dried bird's eye chili
¼ tsp. five-spice powder
9 oz. beef tenderloin
1 tbsp. dark soy sauce
6 scallions
1 carrot

¼ cucumber
8 radishes
1 red onion
¼ head Chinese cabbage
2 tbsp. peanut oil
1 garlic clove, crushed
1 tsp. finely chopped lemon grass
1 tbsp. chopped fresh mint

1 tbsp. chopped fresh cilantro

DRESSING:
3 tbsp. lime juice
1 tbsp. light soy sauce
2 tsp. soft light brown sugar
1 tsp. sesame oil

1 Crush the peppercorns, coriander seeds, and chili in a mortar and pestle, then mix with the five-spice powder and sprinkle on a plate. Brush the beef all over with soy sauce, then roll it in the spices to coat evenly.

2 Cut the scallions into 2½ inch lengths and shred finely lengthways. Place in iced water and leave until curled. Drain well.

3 Trim the carrot and cut into very thin diagonal slices. Halve the cucumber and scoop out the seeds, then slice thinly. Trim the radishes and cut into flower shapes.

4 Slice the onion thinly, cutting each slice from top to root. Roughly shred the Chinese cabbage. Toss all the vegetables together in a large salad bowl.

5 Heat the oil in a heavy-based frying pan and fry the garlic and lemon grass until just turning golden brown. Add the steak and press down with a spatula to ensure it browns evenly. Cook for 3–4 minutes, turning it over once, depending on thickness. Remove the pan from the heat.

6 Slice the steak thinly and toss into the salad with the mint and cilantro. Mix together the dressing ingredients and stir into the pan, then spoon over the salad. Serve immediately.

Desserts & Drinks

The normal end to a Thai meal is a basket of fresh, tropical fruits, often including fragrant mangoes, mangosteens, jackfruit, guavas, lychees, and rambutans. Thai desserts and sweetmeats are mostly made at home for between meal treats, or made by experts and reserved for banquets and special occasions, as their preparation can be time-consuming and often requires skillful blending and shaping.

Even the simplest fruits in sugar syrups are delicately scented with jasmine or rose, usually served with little mouthfuls of sticky rice. Others are poached in coconut milk and sweetened or caramelized with palm sugar.

As in all Thai dishes, the ubiquitous coconut plays a large part in sweet recipes, as coconut milk or cream in sweet custards, in delectable sweet creamy morsels, or delicately scented jellies, or shredded for decoration. Rice, usually of the sticky variety, and tapioca, are vital ingredients in many sweets and cakes, often molded or subtly colored, or soaked in scented syrups or scented with burning incense.

Many Thai drinks are colorful and exotic in flavor, using the abundance of fruits and coconut milk to their best advantage in long, refreshing drinks, sweetened with palm sugar and often with a generous dash of local whisky or other liqueur.

Mangoes in Lemon Grass Syrup

A simple, fresh-tasting fruit dessert to round off a rich meal perfectly.
Serve the mango lightly chilled.

Serves 4

INGREDIENTS

2 large, ripe mangoes
1 lime

1 lemon grass stalk, chopped

3 tbsp. superfine sugar

1 Halve the mangoes, remove the pits, and peel off the skins.

2 Slice the flesh into long, thin slices and arrange them in a shallow layer in a wide serving dish.

3 Remove a few shreds of the rind from the lime for decoration, then cut the lime in half and squeeze out the juice.

4 Place the lime juice in a small pan with the lemon grass and sugar. Heat gently without boiling until the sugar is completely

dissolved. Remove from the heat and allow to cool completly.

5 Strain the cooled syrup into a pitcher and pour evenly over the mango slices. Scatter with the lime rind strips and chill before serving.

COOK'S TIP

To serve this dessert on a hot day, particularly if it is to stand for a while, place the dish on a bed of crushed ice to keep the fruit and syrup chilled.

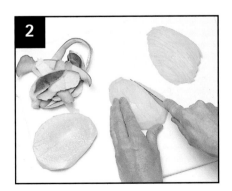

Exotic Fruit Salad

This colorful, exotic salad is infused with the delicate flavors of jasmine tea and ginger.
Ideally, it should be made and chilled about an hour before serving to allow the flavors to develop.

Serves 6

INGREDIENTS

1 tsp. jasmine tea	2 tbsp. superfine sugar	1 starfruit
1tsp. grated fresh ginger root	1 papaya	2 passionfruit
1 strip lime rind	1 mango	
½ cup boiling water	½ small pineapple	

1 Place the tea, ginger, and lime rind in a heatproof cup and pour over the boiling water. Leave to infuse for 5 minutes, then strain the liquid.

2 Add the sugar to the liquid and stir well to dissolve. Leave the syrup until it is completely cool.

3 Halve, deseed, and peel the papaya. Halve the mango, remove the pit, and peel. Peel and remove the core from the pineapple. Cut the fruits into bite-sized pieces.

4 Slice the starfruit crossways. Placc all the prepared fruits in a wide serving bowl and pour over the cooled syrup. Cover with plastic wrap and chill for about 1 hour.

5 Cut the passion-fruit in half, scoop out the flesh and mix with the lime juice. Spoon over the salad and serve.

COOK'S TIP

Starfruit have little flavor when unripe and green, but once ripened and turning yellow they become delicately sweet and fragrant. Usually by this stage, the tips of the ridges have become brown, so you will need to remove these before slicing. The easiest and quickest method of doing this is to run a vegetable peeler along each ridge.

Rose Ice

A delicately perfumed sweet granita ice, which is coarser than many ice creams.
This looks very pretty piled on a glass dish with rose petals scattered around it.

Serves 4

INGREDIENTS

1¾ cups water
2 tbsp. creamed coconut
4 tbsp. sweetened condensed milk

2 tsp. rosewater
a few drops pink food coloring
(optional)

pink rose petals (from an untreated
rose), to decorate,

1 Place the water and creamed coconut in a small pan and heat gently without boiling until the coconut is dissolved.

2 Remove from the heat and allow to cool. Stir in the condensed milk, rosewater, and food coloring (if using). Pour into a freezer container and freeze for 1–1½ hours until slushy.

3 Remove from the freezer, and break up the ice crystals with a fork. Return to the freezer and freeze until firm.

4 Spoon the ice roughly into a pile on a serving dish and scatter with rose petals to serve.

COOK'S TIP

To prevent the ice from thawing too quickly at the table, nestle the base of the serving dish in another dish filled with crushed ice.

Mango & Lime Sorbet

A refreshing sorbet is the perfect way to round off a spicy Thai meal, and mangoes make a deliciously smooth textured, velvety sorbet.

Serves 4

INGREDIENTS

6 tbsp. superfine sugar
scant ½ cup water
finely grated rind of 3 limes

9 tbsp. lime juice
2 tbsp. creamed coconut
2 large, ripe mangoes

curls of toasted fresh coconut, to
decorate

1 Place the sugar, water, and lime rind in a small pan and heat gently, stirring, until the sugar dissolves. Boil rapidly for 2 minutes to reduce slightly, then remove from the heat and strain into a bowl. Stir in the creamed coconut to dissolve and allow to cool.

2 Halve the mangoes, remove the pits, and peel thinly. Chop the flesh roughly and place in a food processor with the lime juice. Process to a smooth purée.

3 Pour the cooled syrup into the mango purée, mixing evenly.

Pour into a freezer container and freeze for 1 hour, or until slushy in texture. (Alternatively, use an electric ice-cream maker.)

4 Remove the container from the freezer and beat with an electric mixer to break up the ice crystals. Refreeze for a further hour, then remove from the freezer and beat again until smooth.

5 Cover the container, return to the freezer, and freeze until firm. To serve, remove from the freezer and leave at room

temperature for about 15 minutes before scooping. Scatter with toasted coconut to serve.

COOK'S TIP

If you prefer, canned mangoes in syrup can be used to make the sorbet. Omit the sugar and water, and infuse the lime rind in the canned syrup instead.

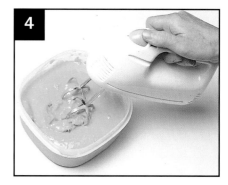

Lychee & Ginger Sorbet

A refreshing palate-cleanser after a rich meal, this sorbet couldn't be easier to make, and can be served either on it's own or as a cooling accompaniment to a fruit salad.

Serves 4

INGREDIENTS

14 oz. cans lychees in syrup
finely grated rind of 1 lime
2 tbsp. lime juice

3 tbsp. candied ginger syrup
2 egg whites

TO DECORATE:
starfruit slices
slivers of candied ginger

1 Drain the lychees, reserving the syrup. Place the fruits in a blender or food processor with the lime rind, juice, and candied ginger syrup and purée until completely smooth.

2 Mix the purée thoroughly with the reserved syrup and pour into a freezerproof container and freeze for 1–1½ hours until slushy in texture. (Alternatively, use an ice-cream maker.)

3 Remove from the freezer and whisk to break up the ice crystals. Whisk the egg whites in a clean, dry bowl until stiff, then quickly and lightly fold into the iced mixture.

4 Return to the freezer and freeze until firm. Serve the sorbet in scoops, with slices of starfruit and ginger to decorate.

COOK'S TIP

It is not recommended that raw egg whites are served to very young children, pregnant women, the elderly or anyone weakened by chronic illness. The egg whites may be left out of this recipe, but you will need to whisk the sorbet a second time after another hour of freezing to obtain a light texture.

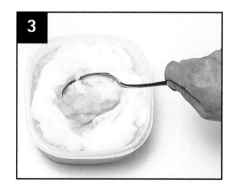

Pineapple with Cardamom & Lime

Thai pineapples are sweet and fragrant, and this local fruit appears regularly as a dessert,
usually served very simply, but always skillfully sliced and carefully presented.

Serves 4

INGREDIENTS

1 pineapple
2 cardamom pods

1 thinly pared strip lime rind
1 tbsp. soft light brown sugar

3 tbsp. lime juice

1 Cut the top and base from the pineapple, cut away the peel and remove the "eyes" from the flesh. Cut into quarters and remove the core. Slice lengthways.

2 Crush the cardamom pods in a mortar and pestle and place in a pan with the lime rind and 4 tablespoons water. Heat until boiling, then simmer for 30 seconds.

3 Remove from the heat and add the sugar, then cover and leave to infuse for 5 minutes.

4 Stir in the sugar to dissolve, add the lime juice, then strain the syrup over the pineapple. Chill for 30 minutes.

5 Arrange the pineapple on a serving dish, spoon over the syrup and serve.

COOK'S TIP

To remove the 'eyes' from pineapple, cut off the peel, then use a small sharp knife to cut a V-shaped channel down the pineapple, cutting diagonally through the lines of brown "eyes" in the flesh, to make spiraling cuts around the fruit.

Coconut Custard Squares

This easy dessert with an exotic flavor is quite sensuous in texture. It is especially luxurious served with a few slivers of mango or papaya on the side.

Serves 4

INGREDIENTS

1 tsp. butter, melted
6 large eggs
1¾ cups coconut milk

¾ cup soft light brown sugar
pinch of salt

shreds of coconut and lime rind, to decorate

1 Brush the butter over the inside of a 7½ inch square buttered ovenproof dish or pan, about 1½ inch deep.

2 Beat the eggs in a large bowl and beat in the coconut milk, sugar, and salt.

3 Place the bowl over a pan of gently simmering water and stir with a wooden spoon for 15 minutes, or until it begins to thicken. Pour into the prepared dish or pan.

4 Bake the custard in a preheated oven at 350° F for 20–25 minutes until just set. Remove from the oven and allow to cool completely.

5 Cut the custard into squares and serve scattered with strips of coconut and lime rind.

COOK'S TIP

Keep and eye on the custard as it bakes, as if it overcooks the texture will be spoiled. When it comes out of the oven it should be barely set and still slightly wobbly in the center, then it will firm up slightly as it cools.

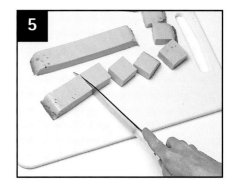

Mung Bean Custards

Mung beans give this sweet custard an unusual texture, and it's a real treat served with a generous dollop of crème fraîche and a squeeze of lime.

Serves 6

INGREDIENTS

1/3 cup dried mung beans
2 large eggs, beaten
3/4 cup coconut milk
1/2 cup superfine sugar

1 tbsp. ground rice
1 tsp. ground cinnamon

TO DECORATE:
fine shreds of lime rind
lime slices
ground cinnamon to sprinkle

1 Place the beans in a saucepan with enough water to cover. Bring to a boil, then lower the heat a simmer for 30–40 minutes until the beans are very tender. Drain well.

2 Mash the beans, then press through a sieve to make a smooth purée.

3 Place the bean purée, eggs, coconut milk, sugar, rice flour, and cinnamon in a large bowl and beat well until thoroughly mixed.

4 Grease and line four 150 ml ramekins and pour in the mixture. Place on a baking sheet in a preheated oven at 350° F and bake for 20–25 minutes until just set.

5 Cool the custards in the molds, then run a knife around the edge to loosen and turn out on to a serving plate. Sprinkle with lime rind and cinnamon, add a twist of lime, and serve with a spoonful of whipped cream or crème fraîche.

COOK'S TIP

Canned mung beans can save time with this dish. Simply omit Step 1, drain the beans thoroughly and rinse in cold water before mashing.

Banana Fritters in Coconut Batter

*This irresistible, classic dessert is best served with a squeeze of lime juice,
and topped with a generous spoonful rich vanilla ice cream.*

Serves 4

INGREDIENTS

9 tbsp. all-purpose flour
2 tbsp. rice flour
1 tbsp. superfine sugar
1 egg, separated

$^2/_3$ cup coconut milk
4 large bananas
sunflower oil for deep frying

TO DECORATE:
1 tsp. powdered sugar
1 tsp. ground cinnamon

1 Sift the all-purpose flour, rice flour, and sugar into a bowl and make a well in the center. Add the egg yolk and coconut milk and beat until a smooth, thick batter forms.

2 Whisk the egg white in a clean, dry bowl until stiff enough to hold soft peaks. Fold it into the batter lightly and evenly.

3 Heat a 2$^1/_2$ inch depth of oil in a large pan to 350° F, or until a cube of bread browns in 30 seconds. Cut the bananas in half

crossways, then dip them quickly into the batter to coat. Drop them carefully into the hot oil and fry in batches for 2–3 minutes until golden brown, turning once.

4 Drain well on paper towels. Sprinkle with powdered sugar and cinnamon, and serve immediately.

COOK'S TIP

If you can buy the baby finger bananas that are popular in this dish in the East, leave them whole for coating and frying.

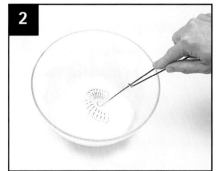

Bananas in Coconut Milk

An unusual dessert which is equally good served hot or cold.
The Thais like to combine fruits and vegetables, so it's not unusual to find
mung beans or sweetcorn mixed with bananas or other fruits.

Serves 4

INGREDIENTS

4 large bananas
1½ cups coconut milk
2 tbsp. superfine sugar

pinch of salt
½ tsp. orange-flower water

1 tbsp. chopped fresh mint
2 tbsp. cooked mung beans

1 Peel the bananas and cut them into short chunks. Place in a large pan with the coconut milk, superfine sugar, and salt.

2 Heat gently until boiling and simmer for 1 minute. Remove from the heat.

3 Sprinkle the orange-flower water over, stir in the mint and spoon into a serving dish.

4 Place the mung beans in a heavy-based pan and place over a high heat until turning crisp and golden, shaking the pan occasionally. Remove and crush lightly in a pestle and mortar.

5 Sprinkle the toasted beans over the bananas and serve warm or cold.

COOK'S TIP

If you prefer, the mung beans could be replaced with flaked, toasted almonds or hazelnuts.

Caramel Apple Wedges with Sesame Seeds

A Thai version of a Chinese dessert, these sweet caramel-coated pieces of fruit take practice to perfect, but the trick is to get the timing right. Bananas can also be cooked in this way.

Serves 4

INGREDIENTS

1 cup rice flour
1 medium egg
½ cup cold water

4 crisp dessert apples
2½ tbsp. sesame seeds
1¼ cups superfine sugar

2 tbsp. vegetable oil
extra vegetable oil for deep frying

1 Place the flour, egg, and water in a bowl and whisking well until a smooth, thick batter forms.

2 Core the apples and cut each into 8 wedges. Drop into the batter and stir in the sesame seeds.

3 Place the sugar and 2 tablespoons oil in a heavy-based pan. Heat, stirring, until the sugar dissolves. Stir until the syrup just begins to turn golden. Remove from the heat but keep warm.

4 Heat the oil in a wok or deep pan to 350° F, or until a cube of bread turns golden in 30 seconds. Lift the apple pieces one by one from the batter, using chopsticks or tongs, lower into the hot oil.

5 Fry for 2–3 minutes until golden brown and crisp. Remove with a perforated spoon and dip very quickly into the sugar mixture. Dip briefly into iced water and drain on waxed paper. Serve immediately.

COOK'S TIP

Take care not to overheat the sugar syrup or it will become difficult to handle and burn. If it begins to set before you have finished dipping the apple pieces, warm it slightly over the heat until it becomes liquid again.

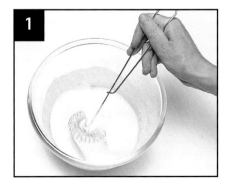

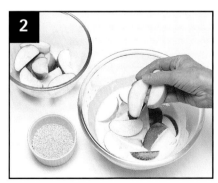

Thai Rice Pudding

*This Thai-style version of rice pudding is mildly spiced and creamy, with a rich custard topping.
It's excellent served warm, and even better the next day served cold –
in Thailand it's even served for breakfast.*

Serves 4

INGREDIENTS

½ cup short-grain rice
2 tbsp. palm (or dark brown) sugar
1 cardamom pod, split
1¼ cups coconut milk

⅔ cup water
3 medium eggs
scant 1 cup coconut cream
1½ tbsp. superfine sugar

fresh fruit, to serve
sweetened coconut flakes, to decorate

1 Place the rice and palm sugar in a pan. Crush the seeds from the cardamom pod in mortar and pestle, and add to the pan. Stir in the coconut milk and water.

2 Bring to a boil, stirring to dissolve the sugar. Lower the heat and simmer, uncovered, stirring occasionally for about 20 minutes until the rice is tender and most of the liquid is absorbed.

3 Pour the rice into 4 individual ovenproof dishes and spread

evenly. Place the dishes in a wide roasting pan with water to come about halfway up the sides.

4 Beat together the eggs, coconut cream, and superfine sugar, and spoon over the rice,. Cover with foil and bake in an oven preheated to 350° F for 45–50 minutes until the custard sets.

5 Serve the rice puddings warm or cold, with fresh fruit and decorated with coconut flakes.

COOK'S TIP

Cardamom is quite a powerful spice, so if you find it too strong it can be left out altogether, or replaced with a little ground cinnamon.

Sticky Rice Balls

Glutinous rice is the base for many Thai desserts, and these little rice balls are typical.
They're often prettily colored with food colorings and soaked in flower-scented syrups,
and children love them.

Serves 4

INGREDIENTS

1½ cups glutinous (sticky) rice
pink and green food colorings

2½ cups granulated sugar
1¼ cups water

few drops of rose water or jasmine
essence

1 Place the rice in a bowl and add enough cold water to cover. Leave to soak for 3 hours, or overnight.

2 Drain the rice and rinse thoroughly in cold water.

3 Line the top part of a steamer with cheesecloth and pour the rice into it. Place over boiling water, cover and steam the rice for 30 minutes. Remove and cool.

4 Heat the sugar and water gently until the sugar

dissolves. Bring to a boil and boil for 4-5 minutes to reduce to a thin syrup. Remove the pan from the heat.

5 Divide the rice in half and color one half pale pink, the other half pale green. Shape into small balls.

6 Using 2 forks, dip the rice balls into the syrup, drain off the excess, and pile onto a dish. Scatter with rose petals or jasmine flowers.

COOK'S TIP

If you prefer, the rice balls can be shaped in small molds like dariole molds as seen in the photo at right.

Balinese Banana Pancakes

*These little stacks of rich banana pancakes, drizzled with fragrant lime juice,
are quite irresistible any time of day!*

Serves 6

INGREDIENTS

1¼ cups all-purpose flour
pinch of salt
4 medium eggs, beaten
2 large, ripe bananas, peeled and
   mashed

1¼ cups coconut milk
vegetable oil for frying
sliced banana, to decorate
6 tbsp. lime juice

powdered sugar
coconut cream, to serve

1 Place the flour, salt, eggs, bananas, and coconut milk in a blender or food processor and process until a smooth batter forms. Alternatively, if you don't have a food processor, sift the flour and salt into a bowl and make a well in the center, then add the remaining ingredients and beat well until smooth.

2 Chill the batter in the refrigerator for about an hour. Remove and beat briefly again. Heat a small amount of oil in a small frying pan until very hot.

3 Drop tablespoonfuls of batter into the pan. Cook until golden underneath, then turn and cook the other side until golden brown.

4 Cook in batches until all the batter is used up, making about 36 pancakes. Remove and drain on paper towels. Serve the pancakes in a stack, decorated with sliced bananas and sprinkled with lime juice and icing sugar. Serve with coconut cream.

COOK'S TIP

These little pancakes are best eaten hot and freshly cooked, so keep them hot in a low oven while the others are cooking.

Coconut Crepes

These pretty, lacy-thin crepes are sold by Thai street vendors, often colored a delicate pale pink, or tinted green with the juice from pandanus leaves. Add a tiny drop of food color if you like, but they look pretty good just as they are, especially served with fresh fruits.

Serves 4

INGREDIENTS

1 cup rice flour
3 tbsp. superfine sugar
pinch of salt
2 medium eggs

2½ cups coconut milk
4 tbsp. shredded coconut
vegetable oil for frying
fresh mango or banana, to serve

2 tbsp. palm (or dark brown) sugar, to decorate

1 Place the rice flour, sugar, and salt in a bowl and add the eggs and coconut milk, whisking until a smooth batter forms. Alternatively, place all the ingredients in a blender and process to a smooth batter. Beat in half the coconut.

2 Heat a small amount of oil in a wide, heavy-based frying pan. Pour in a little batter, swirling the pan to cover the surface thinly and evenly. Cook until pale golden underneath.

3 Turn or toss the pancake and cook quickly to brown lightly on the other side.

4 Turn out and keep hot while making the remaining batter into pancakes.

5 Serve the pancakes folded or loosely rolled, with slices of mango or banana, and sprinkled with palm sugar and the remaining coconut, toasted.

COOK'S TIP

Rice flour gives the pancakes a light, smooth texture, but if it's not available use ordinary all-purpose flour instead.

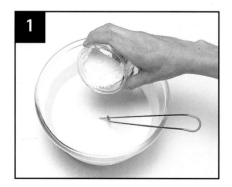

Steamed Coconut Cake with Lime and Ginger Syrup

This steamed coconut cake is very typical of Thai desserts and sweets, and has a distinctly Chinese influence. Eat it in small squares as it's quite rich and sweet.

Serves 8

INGREDIENTS

2 large eggs, separated
pinch of salt
½ cup superfine sugar
5 tbsp. butter, melted and cooled
5 tbsp. coconut milk

1¼ cups self-rising flour
½ tsp. baking powder
3 tbsp. shredded coconut
4 tbsp. candied ginger syrup
3 tbsp. lime juice

TO DECORATE:
3 pieces candied ginger
curls of grated fresh coconut

1 Cut an 11 inch round of nonstick paper and press into a 7 inch steamer basket to line it.

2 Whisk the egg whites with the salt until stiff. Gradually whisk in the sugar 1 tablespoon at a time, whisking hard after each addition until the mixture stands in stiff peaks.

3 Whisk in the yolks, then quickly stir in the butter and coconut milk. Sift the flour and baking powder over the mixture, then fold in lightly and evenly with a large metal spoon. Fold in the coconut.

4 Spoon the mixture into the lined steamer basket and tuck the spare paper over the top. Place the basket over boiling water, cover and steam for 30 minutes.

5 Turn out the cake on to a plate, remove the paper, and cool slightly. Mix together the ginger and lime juice and spoon over the cake. Cut into squares and decorate with diced preserved, candied ginger and curls of fresh coconut.

Strings of Gold

These golden egg threads take a little practice, but they're a very traditional Thai dessert, so well worth a try. The little coils of threads are meant to represent the hands put together in a traditional Thai greeting. The Thai's use a special tool to drizzle the egg in fine streams, but you can use a piping bag.

Serves 4

INGREDIENTS

7 egg yolks
1 tbsp. egg white

2½ cups granulated sugar
scant 1 cup water

handful of scented jasmine flowers
(be sure they are untreated)

1 Press the egg yolks and egg white through a fine sieve, then whisk lightly.

2 Place the sugar and water in a large pan and heat gently until the sugar dissolves. Add the jasmine flowers, bring to a boil and boil rapidly until a thin syrup forms. Remove the flowers with a perforated spoon.

3 Bring the syrup to the simmering point. Using a piping bag with a fine nozzle, or a paper icing cone, quickly drizzle the egg mixture into the syrup in a thin steam to form loose nests or pyramid shapes.

4 As soon as the threads set, remove the nests carefully and drain well on paper towels. Arrange on a warmed serving dish. Garnish with fresh fruit.

COOK'S TIP

If you can't get hold of fresh, scented jasmine flowers, add a few drops of rosewater or orange-flower water to the syrup instead.

Melon & Ginger Crush

A really refreshing summer drink, this melon crush is quick and simple to make.
If you can't buy kaffir limes, ordinary lime are fine.

Serves 4

INGREDIENTS

1 melon, about 1 lb. 12 oz	3 tbsp. kaffir lime juice	1 lime
6 tbsp. ginger ale	crushed ice	

1 Peel, deseed and roughly chop the melon. Place it in a blender or food processor with the ginger ale and lime juice.

2 Blend together on high speed until the mixture is completely smooth.

3 Put plenty of crushed ice into 4 tall tumblers. Pour the the melon and ginger mash over the ice.

4 Cut the lime into slim wedges, cut a slit in each one and slip it on to the side of each glass. Add a slice of lime to each glass as well. Serve immediately.

VARIATION

If your prefer a non-alcoholic version of this drink, simply omit the ginger wine, then top up with ginger ale in the glass. For a change of flavor, use a watermelon when they are in season. Ginger wine is available from specialist wine merchants or liquor stores.

Mango & Coconut Smoothie

A velvety-smooth, delicately scented drink.
This can be served at any time of day—especially for breakfast.

Serves 4

INGREDIENTS

2 large, ripe mangoes	2¼ cups coconut milk	shredded, toasted coconut, to serve
1 tbsp. powdered sugar	5 ice cubes	

1 Cut the mangoes in half and remove the pit. Cut away the peel and coarsley chop the flesh.

2 Place the chopped flesh in a blender or food processor with the powdered sugar and blend until completely smooth.

3 Add the coconut milk and ice to the blender or food processor and blend again until frothy.

4 Pour into 4 tall glasses and sprinkle with shredded, toasted coconut to serve.

COOK'S TIP

To add a special kick to the cocktail (though not perhaps for breakfast!), add a generous dash of white rum to the blender with the coconut milk.

VARIATION

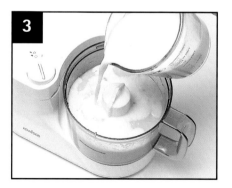

If you don't have shredded, toasted coconut, sprinkle with ground ginger just before serving.

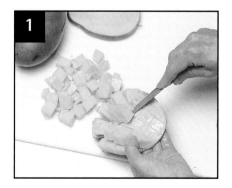

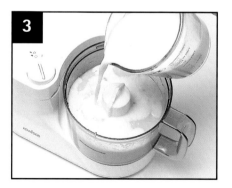

Lime & Lemon Grass Cooler

This cooling, nonalcoholic cocktail looks delightful served in tall glasses with frosted rims. If you're after something stronger, add a shot of gin or vodka to each glass.

Serves 4

INGREDIENTS

egg white and superfine sugar for frosting	1 small lemon grass stalk	½ cup water
2 limes	3 tbsp. superfine sugar	4 extra lime slices
	4 ice cubes	soda water

1 To frost the rim of the glasses, pour a little egg white★ into a saucer. Dip the rim of each glass briefly into egg white and then into superfine sugar.

2 Cut the each lime into 8 pieces and coarsely chop the lemon grass. Place the lime pieces and lemon grass in a blender or food processor with the sugar and ice cubes.

3 Add the water and process for a few seconds, but not until completely smooth.

4 Strain the mixture into the frosted glasses. Add a lime slice to each glass and top up to taste with soda water. Serve immediately.

★Use pasteurized egg products, available where eggs are sold, to avoid the risk of contaminated eggs.

COOK'S TIP

It's important not to blend the limes for too long—a few seconds is enough to finely chop them and extract the juice. If you process too far, the drink will have a bitter flavor.

Thai Cocktail Sling

A Thai-style version of a classic cocktail, this is a long drink with a hefty kick of whisky.

Serves 1

INGREDIENTS

2 tbsp. whisky

1 tbsp. cherry brandy

1 tbsp. orang-flavored liqueur

1 tbsp. lime juice

1 tsp. palm (or dark brown) sugar

dash of Angostura bitters

2 ice cubes

½ cup pineapple juice

1 small wedge pineapple

sprig of fresh mint

1 Place the whisky, cherry brandy, liqueur, lime juice, palm sugar, and Angostura bitters in a cocktail shaker. Shake well to mix thoroughly.

2 Place the ice cubes in a large glass. Pour the cocktail mixture over the ice, then top up with the pineapple juice.

3 Cut a slit in the pineapple wedge and place on the edge of the glass. Top with a sprig of mint and serve immediately.

COOK'S TIP

If the pineapple juice is quite sweet, as Thai pineapple juice is, you may not need to add sugar. So if you're unsure, taste first.

COOK'S TIP

Scotch whisky is very highly regarded in Thailand, although a powerful whisky is distilled locally—if you have the stomach for it!

Tropical Fruit Punch

This exotic-looking cocktail is simplicity itself, and can be varied with different fruit juices.
Top with lavish amounts of fruit for a really festive effect.

Serves 6

INGREDIENTS

1 small ripe mango	1¼ cups orange juice	TO DECORATE:
4 tbsp. lime juice	1¼ cups pineapple juice	orange slices
1 tsp. finely grated fresh ginger	scant ½ cup rum	lime slices
1 tbsp. soft light brown sugar	crushed ice	pineapple slices
		starfruit

1 Peel and pit the mango and chop the flesh. Place in a blender or food processor with the lime juice, ginger, and sugar and process until smooth.

2 Add the orange and pineapple juice and rum and process again until blended.

3 Pour over crushed ice and decorate with slices of orange, lime, pineapple, and starfruit.

COOK'S TIP

To extend the drink a little further, and bring out the ginger flavor more, top up each glass with a generous dash of ginger ale.

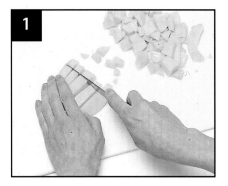